HEATHCLIFF
KOOL KAT

The funniest feline in America delights millions of fans every day as he appears in over 500 newspapers. You'll have a laugh a minute as Heathcliff tangles with the milkman, the cat show judge, the veterinarian and just about everyone else he runs into. If you're looking for some fun, look no further. Heathcliff is here!

Heathcliff Books

HEATHCLIFF
HEATHCLIFF RIDES AGAIN
HEATHCLIFF TRIPLE THREAT
HEATHCLIFF WANTED
HEATHCLIFF SPINS A YARN
HEATHCLIFF DOES IT AGAIN!
HEATHCLIFF STRIKES AGAIN!
HEATHCLIFF ROUND 3
HEATHCLIFF PIGS OUT
HEATHCLIFF FIRST PRIZE!
HEATHCLIFF'S TREASURE CHEST OF PUZZLES
HEATHCLIFF'S PUZZLERS
HEATHCLIFF PUZZLE SLEUTH
HEATHCLIFF BANQUET
HEATHCLIFF FEAST
SWEET SAVAGE HEATHCLIFF
WICKED LOVING HEATHCLIFF
HEATHCLIFF IN CONCERT
HEATHCLIFF PLAY BY PLAY
HEATHCLIFF DINES OUT
HEATHCLIFF GONE FISHIN'
HEATHCLIFF CLEANS HOUSE
HEATHCLIFF WORKING OUT
HEATHCLIFF CATCH OF THE DAY
HEATHCLIFF ON VACATION
HEATHCLIFF KOOL KAT
HEATHCLIFF ROCKIN' AND ROLLIN'
HEATHCLIFF SMOOTH SAILING
HEATHCLIFF ALL AMERICAN
HEATHCLIFF TOP SECRET
HEATHCLIFF CHAIRMAN OF THE BOARD
HEATHCLIFF DOG DAYS

HEATHCLIFF
KOOL KAT

by
Geo Gately

JOVE BOOKS, NEW YORK

Cartoons previously published in
Heathcliff Feast

HEATHCLIFF KOOL KAT

A Jove Book / published by arrangement with
McNaught Syndicate, Inc.

PRINTING HISTORY
Charter Special Book Club edition / August 1986
Jove edition / April 1987

All rights reserved.
Copyright © 1974, 1975, 1981, 1985, 1986 by McNaught
Syndicate, Inc.
This book may not be reproduced in whole or in part,
by mimeograph or any other means, without permission.
For information address: The Berkley Publishing Group,
200 Madison Avenue, New York, New York 10016.

ISBN: 0-515-09148-0

Jove Books are published by The Berkley Publishing Group,
200 Madison Avenue, New York, New York 10016.
The name "JOVE" and the "J" logo
are trademarks belonging to Jove Publications, Inc.

PRINTED IN THE UNITED STATES OF AMERICA

10 9 8 7 6 5 4 3 2

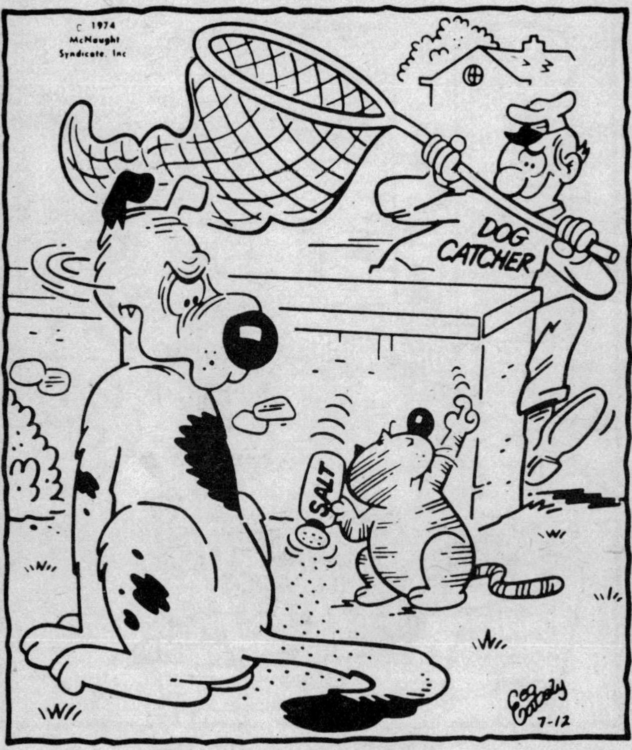
© 1974
McNaught
Syndicate, Inc
DOG
CATCHER
SALT
7-12

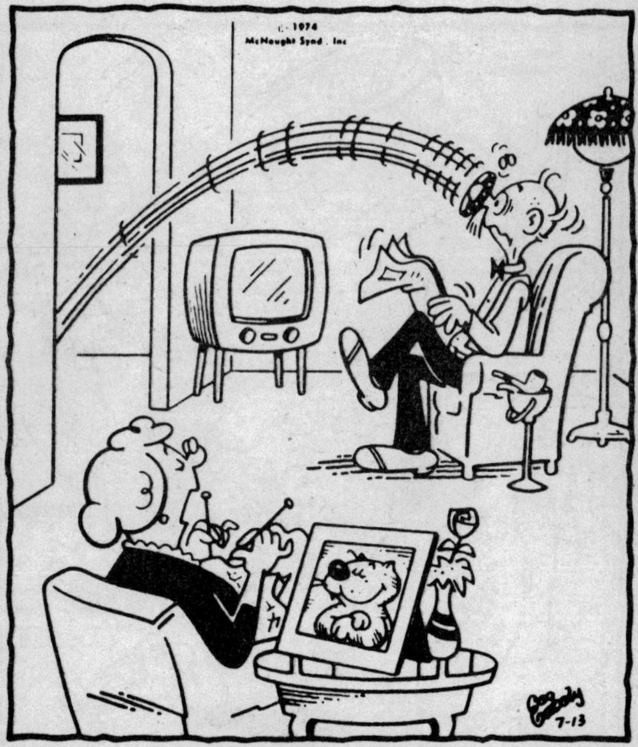
© 1974
McNaught Synd., Inc
7-13

"I DON'T THINK HEATHCLIFF LIKES HIS NEW COLLAR."

"HEATHCLIFF IS IN THE MIDST OF ANOTHER TRIANGLE."

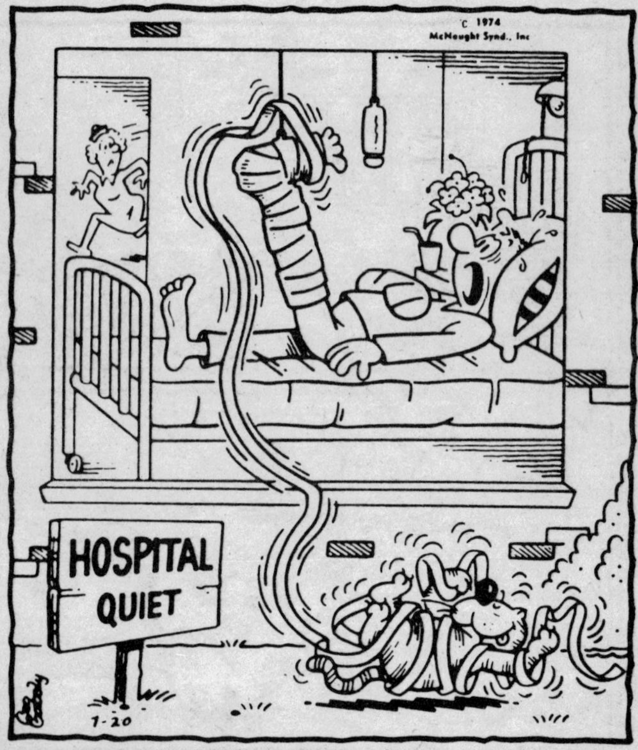
c 1974
McNaught Synd., Inc
HOSPITAL
QUIET
7-20

"HELP!"

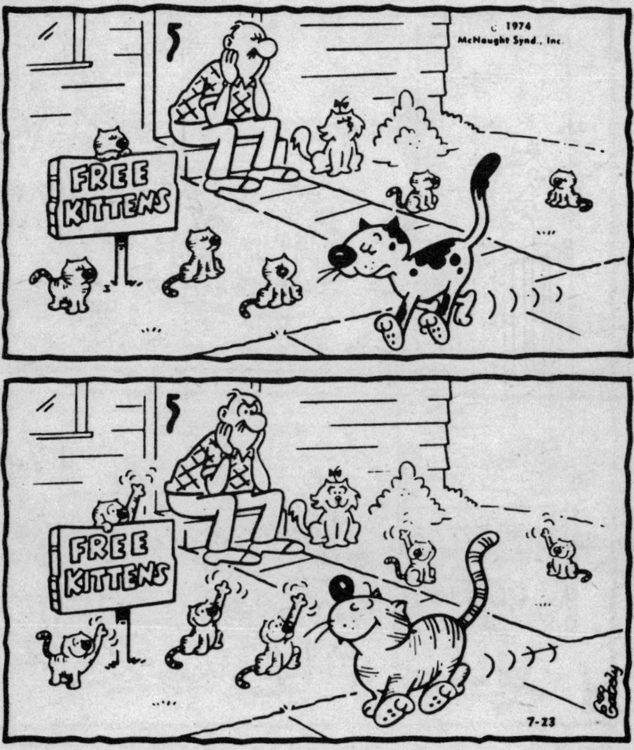
© 1974
McNaught Synd., Inc.
5
FREE
KITTENS
5
FREE
KITTENS
7-23

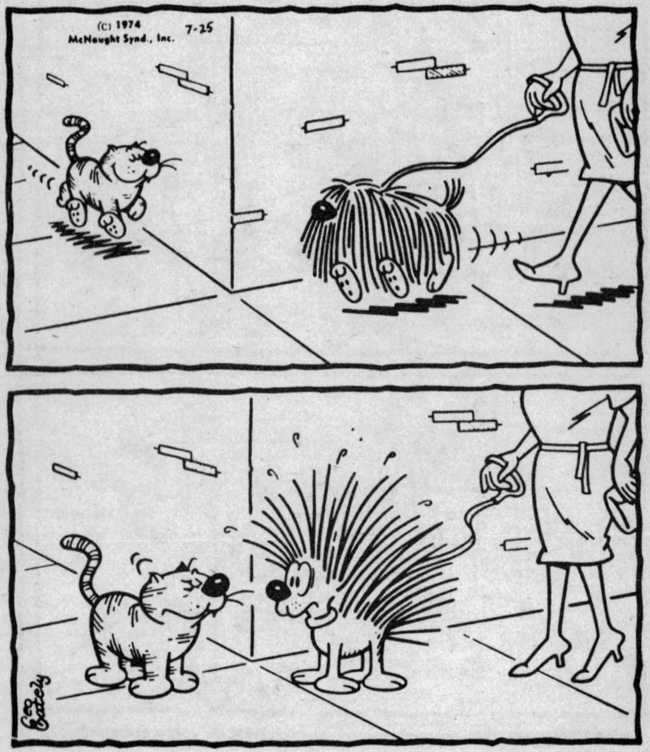
(C) 1974
McNaught Synd., Inc.
7-25
Gately

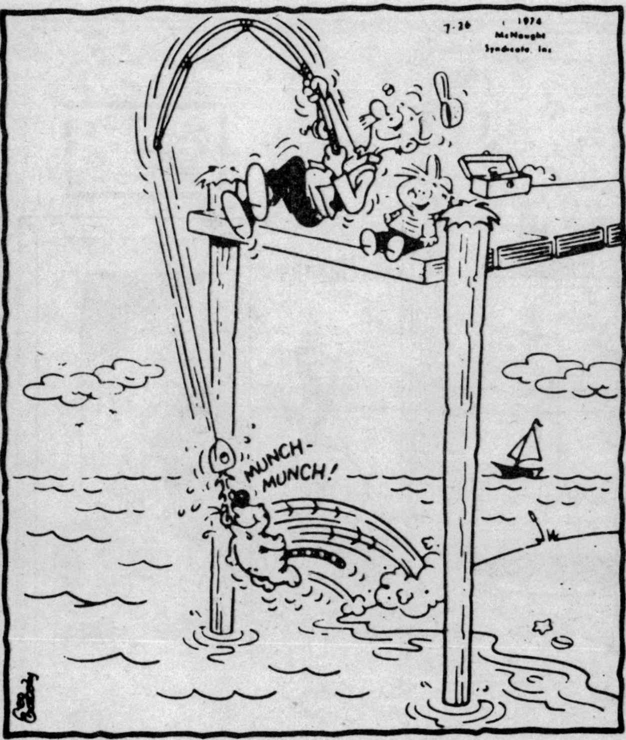
7-26 © 1974 McNaught Syndicate, Inc
MUNCH-
MUNCH!

"WOW!... IT MUST BE A WHOPPER, GRAMPS!"

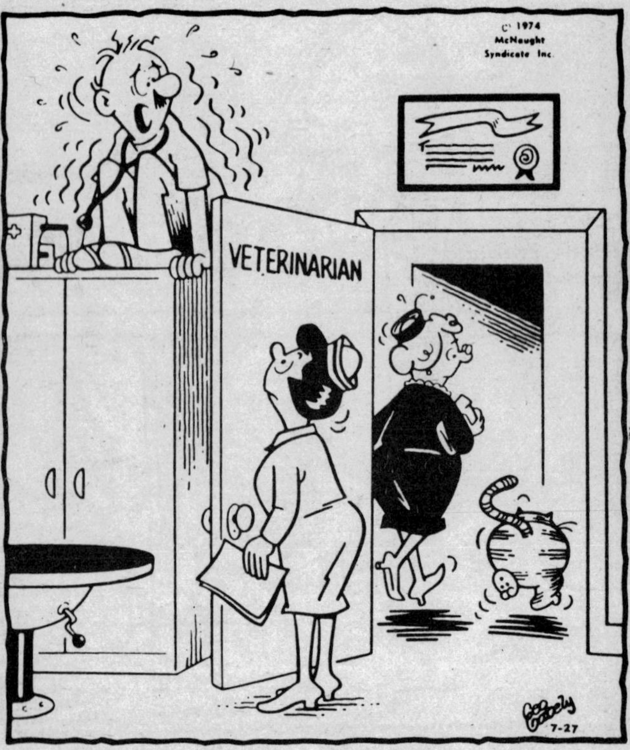
© 1974
McNaught
Syndicate Inc.
VETERINARIAN
7-27
"HAS HE GONE?!"

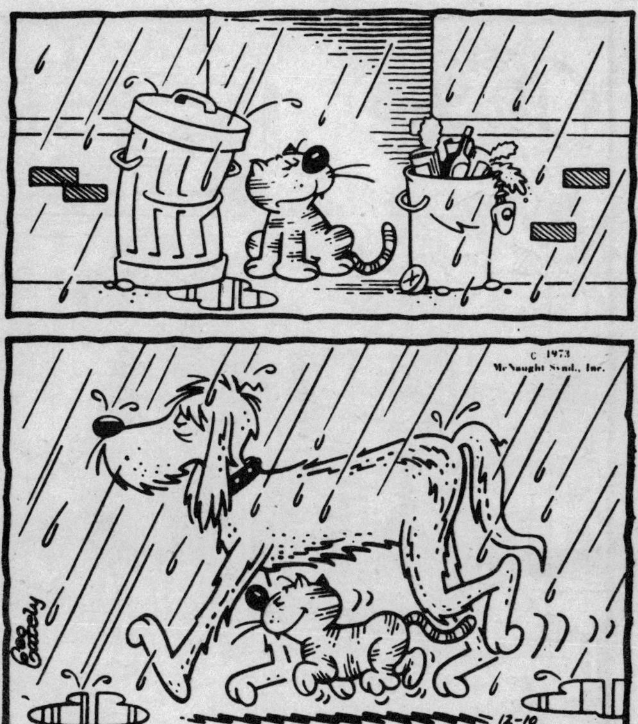
c 1973
McNaught Synd., Inc.
12-10

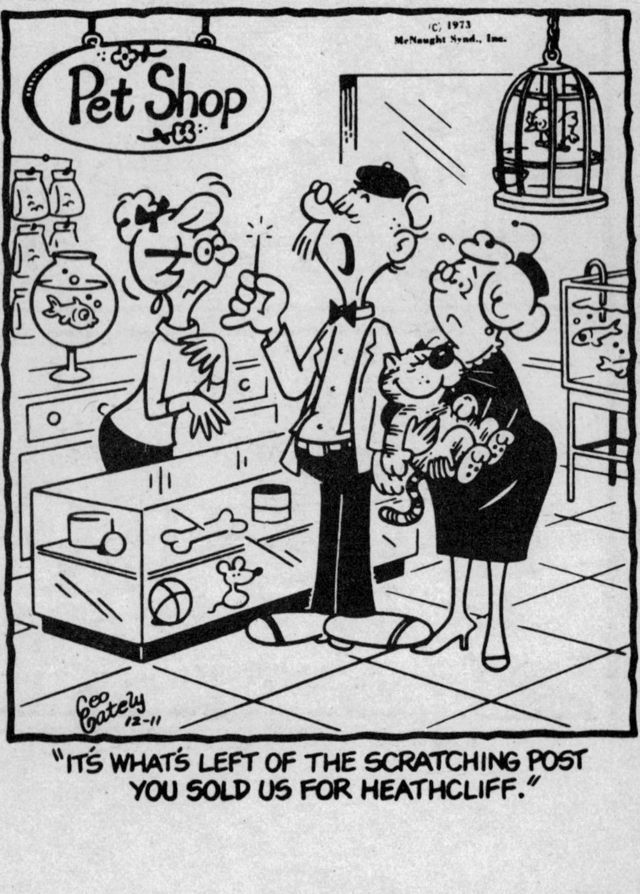
(C) 1973
McNaught Synd., Inc.
Pet Shop
Geo Gately
12-11

"IT'S WHAT'S LEFT OF THE SCRATCHING POST YOU SOLD US FOR HEATHCLIFF."

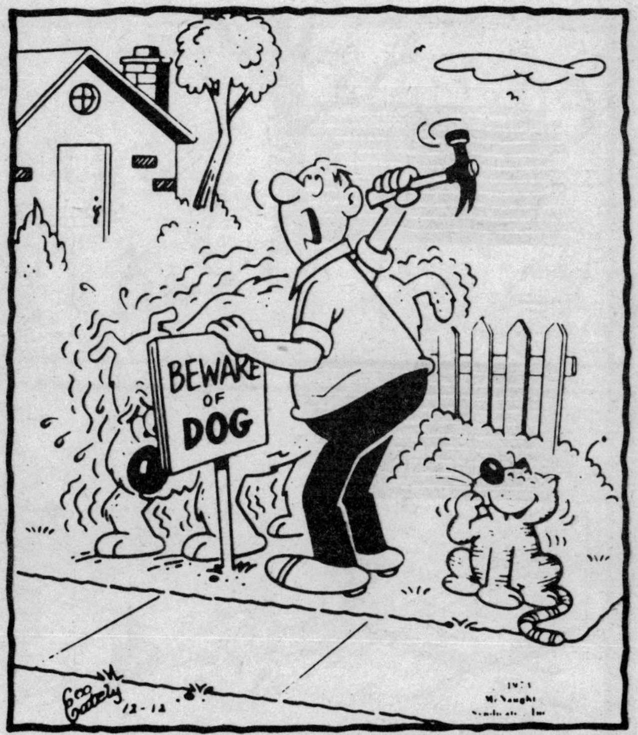
BEWARE OF DOG

"I KEEP HEARING SNICKERING!"

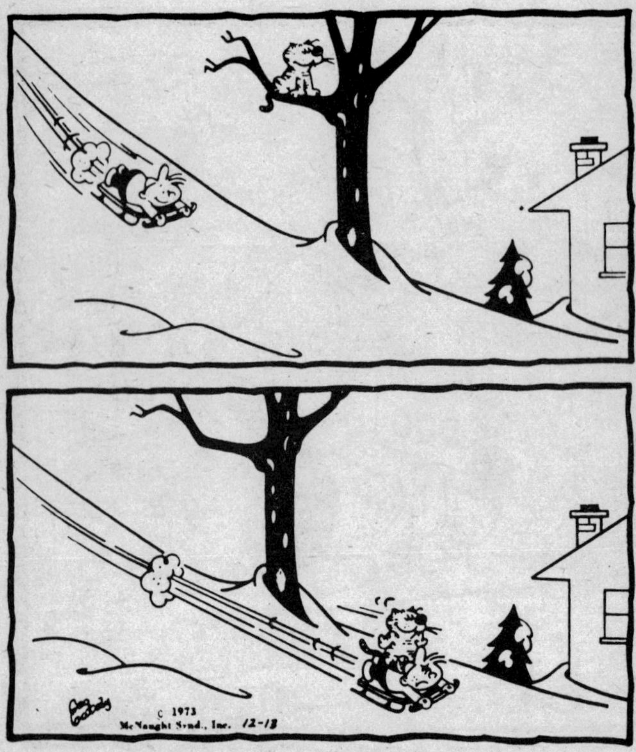
© 1973
McNaught Synd., Inc. 12-13

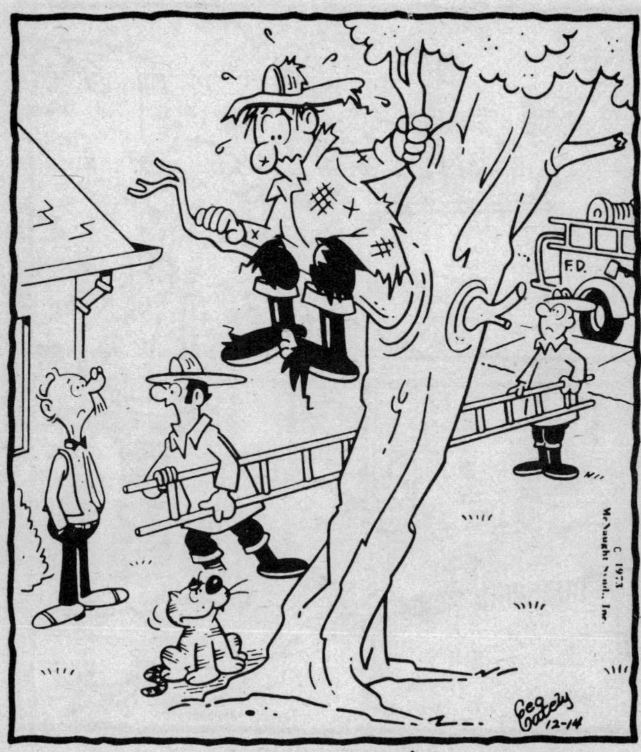
F.D.

"THIS IS THE FIRST TIME WE'VE EVER BEEN CALLED TO GET A FIREMAN OUT OF A TREE!"

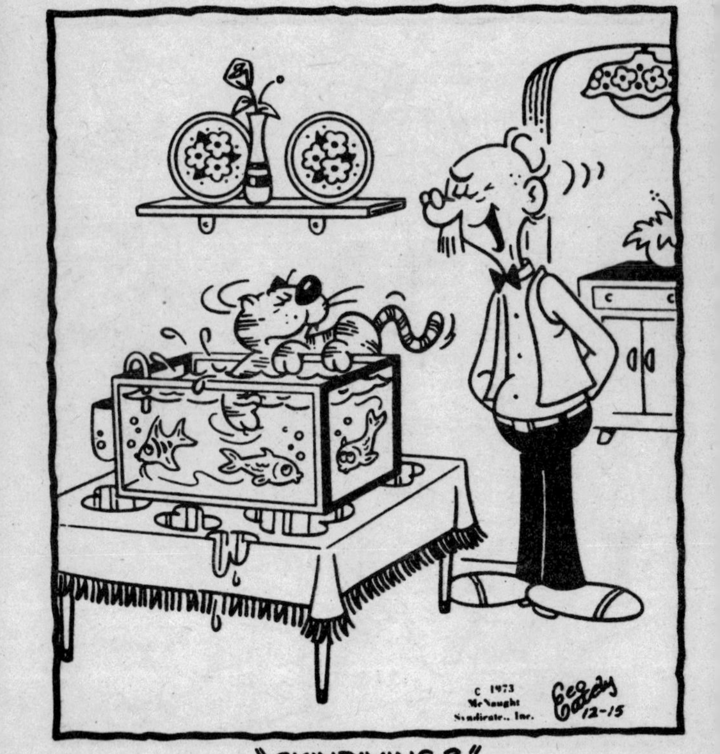
c 1973
McNaught
Syndicate., Inc.
12-15

"SKINDIVING?"

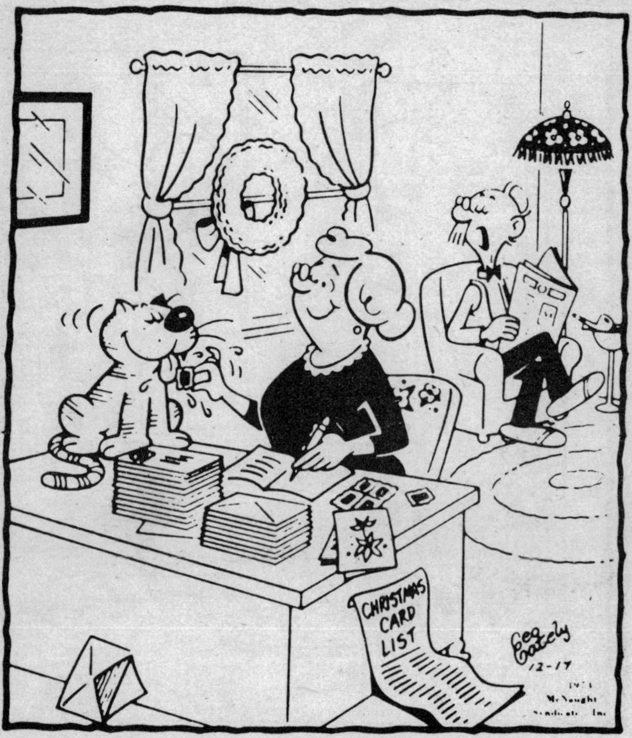
CHRISTMAS CARD LIST
Geo Gately
12-17

"I KNEW HE HAD TO BE GOOD FOR SOMETHING."

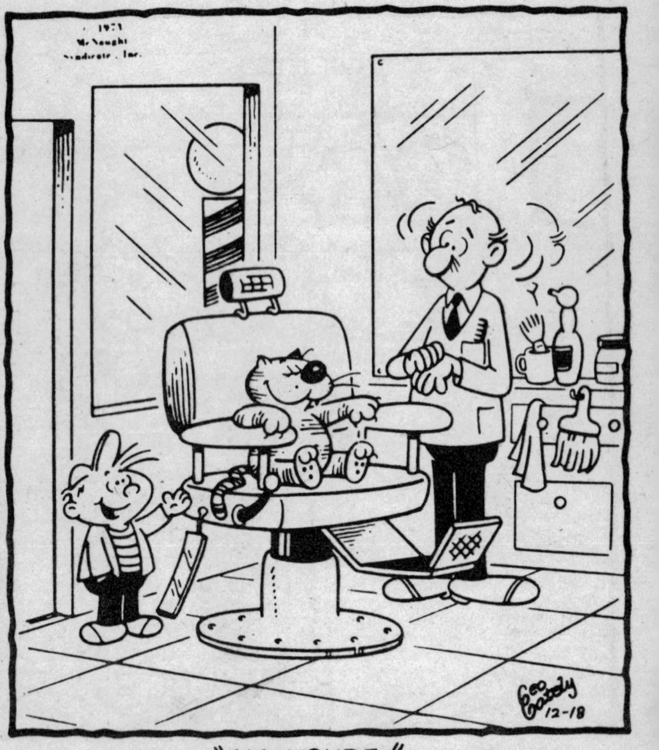
Geo Gately
12-18

"MANICURE."

"HAVE YOU SEEN A LARGE, STRIPED TOM-CAT?"

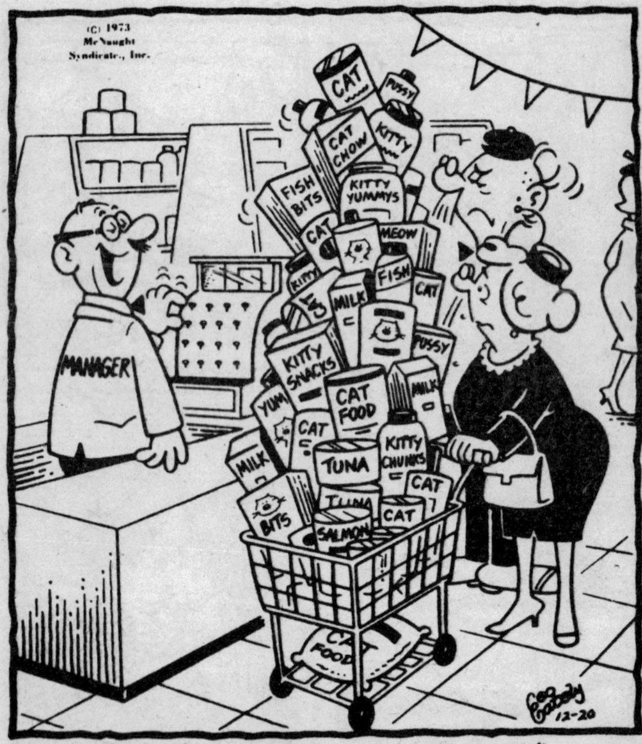
(C) 1973
McNaught
Syndicate, Inc.
CAT
PUSSY
CAT CHOW
KITTY
FISH BITS
KITTY YUMMYS
CAT
MEOW
FISH
CAT
MILK
KITTY SNACKS
PUSSY
MANAGER
YUM
CAT FOOD
MILK
CAT
KITTY CHUNKS
MILK
TUNA
CAT
BITS
CAT
SALMON
CAT FOOD
12-20

"HOW'S GOOD OL' HEATHCLIFF?"

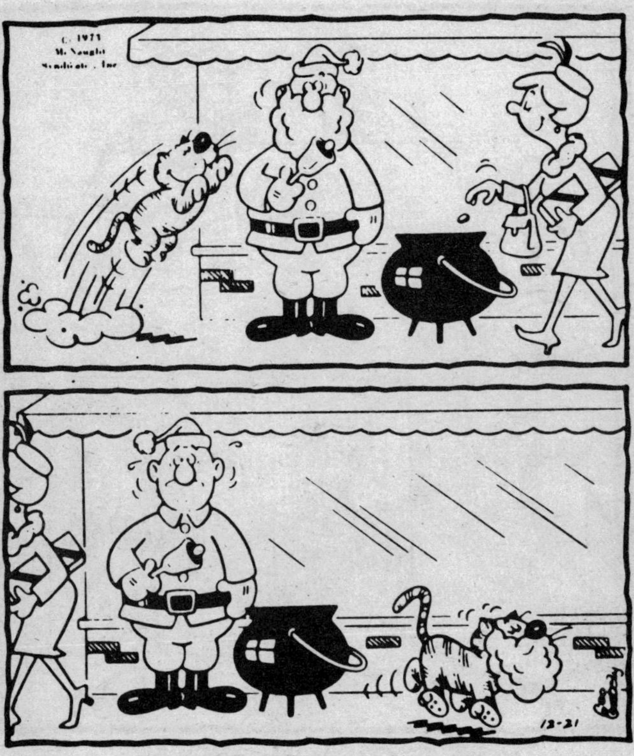

12-21

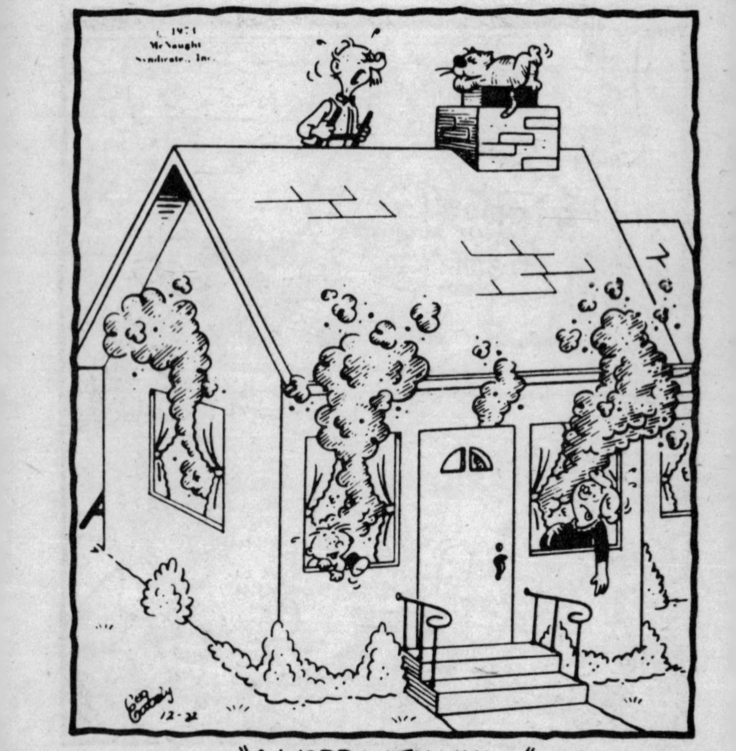
McNaught
Syndicate, Inc.

"A WORD WITH YOU..."

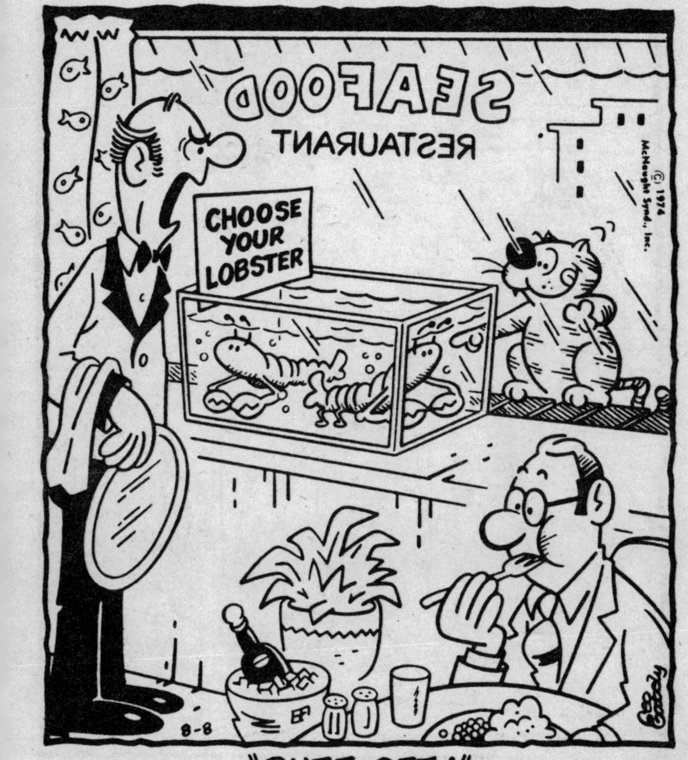
SEAFOOD
RESTAURANT
CHOOSE YOUR LOBSTER
© 1974 McNaught Synd., Inc.
8-8

"BUZZ OFF!"

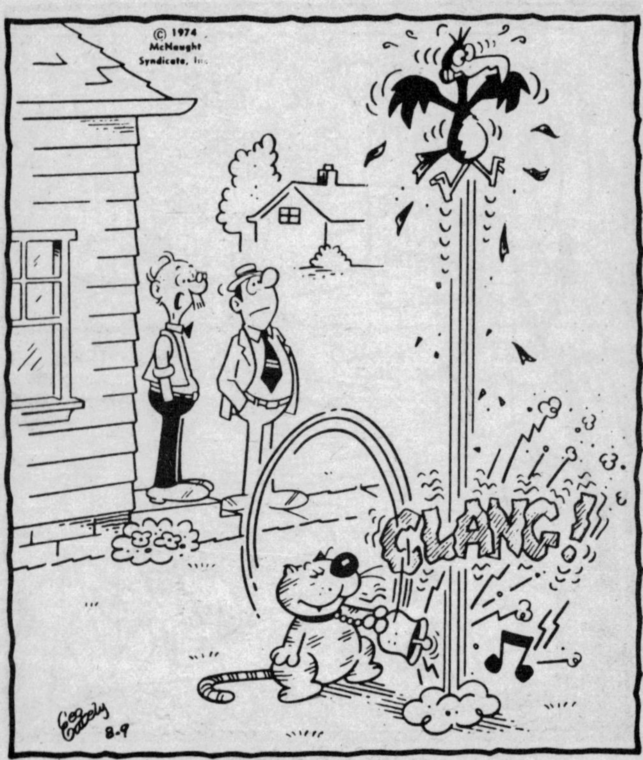
© 1974
McNaught
Syndicate, Inc.
CLANG!!
8-9

"I PUT A BELL ON HEATHCLIFF TO KEEP HIM FROM SNEAKING UP ON BIRDS!"

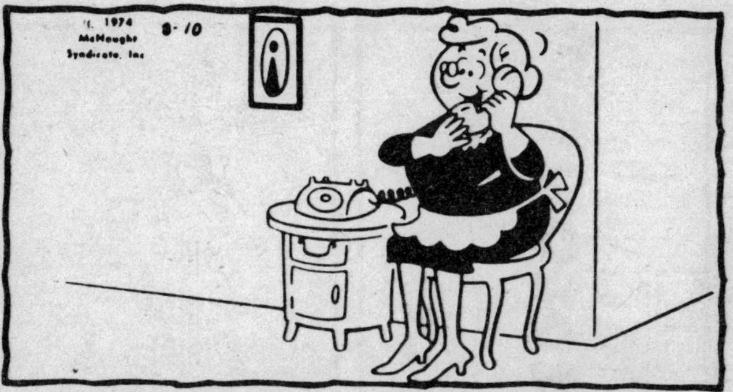
© 1974 McNaught Syndicate, Inc
8-10

"HELLO EMMA?...WAIT 'TIL I GIVE YOU THE LATEST ABOUT RUTHIE!...I TELL YOU IT'S A...

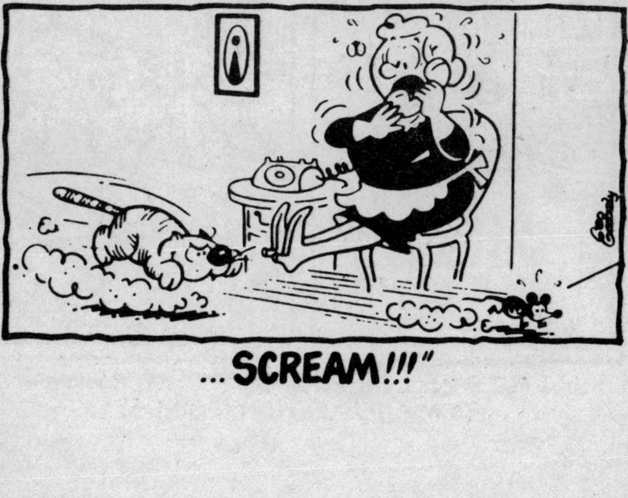

...SCREAM!!!"

EEYOWOWOWOWOW
ECHO CANYON
ECHO CANYON
© 1974 McNaught Synd., Inc.
8-13

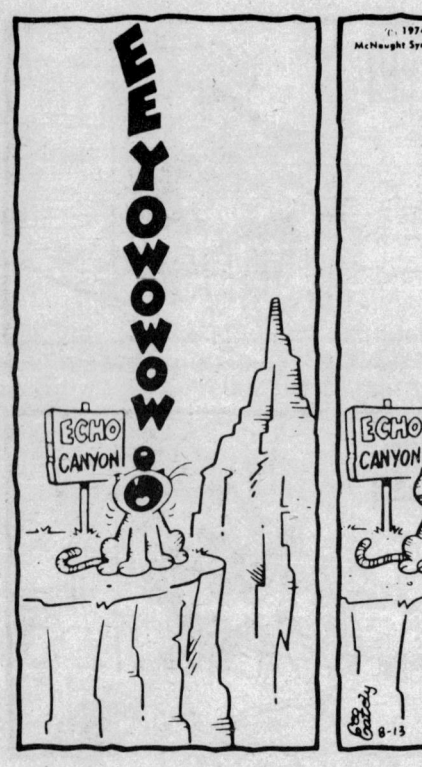

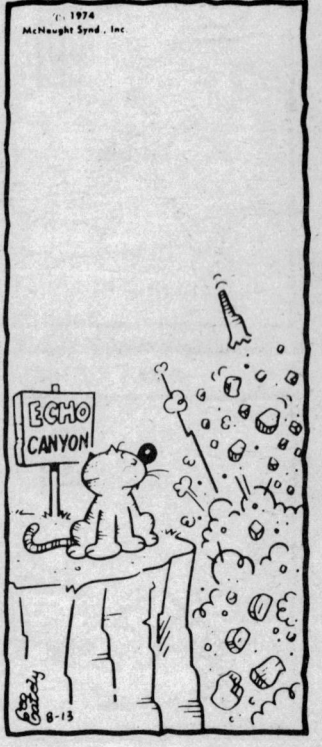

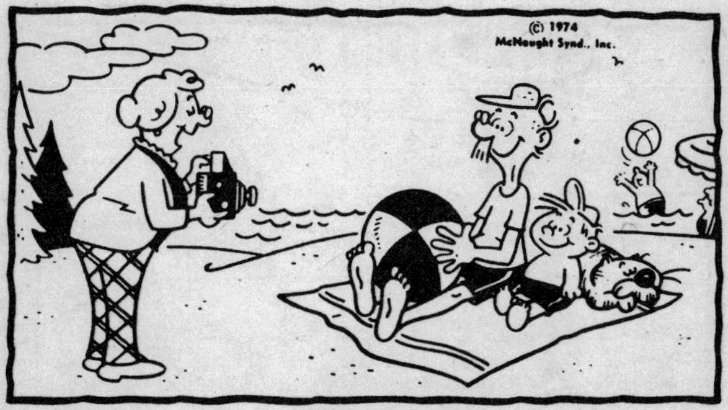
(C) 1974
McNaught Synd., Inc.

"SMILE."

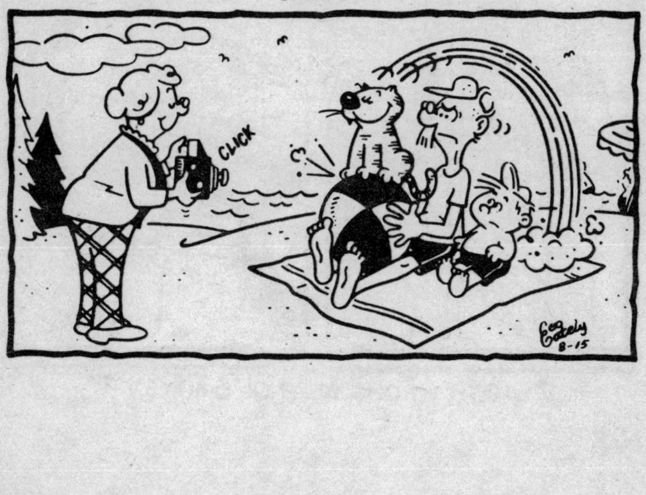
CLICK
Geo Gately
8-15

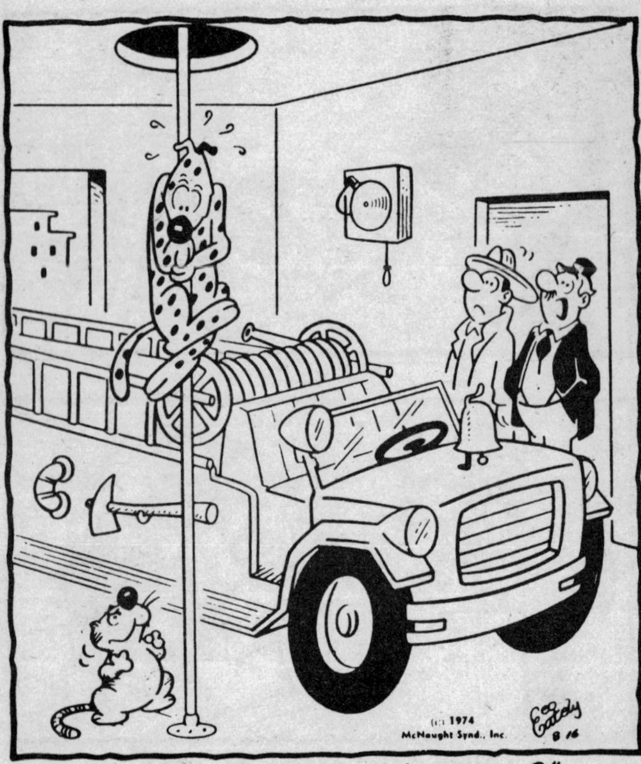
(c) 1974
McNaught Synd., Inc.
8/16

"WHAT'S WRONG WITH OL' SMOKEY?"

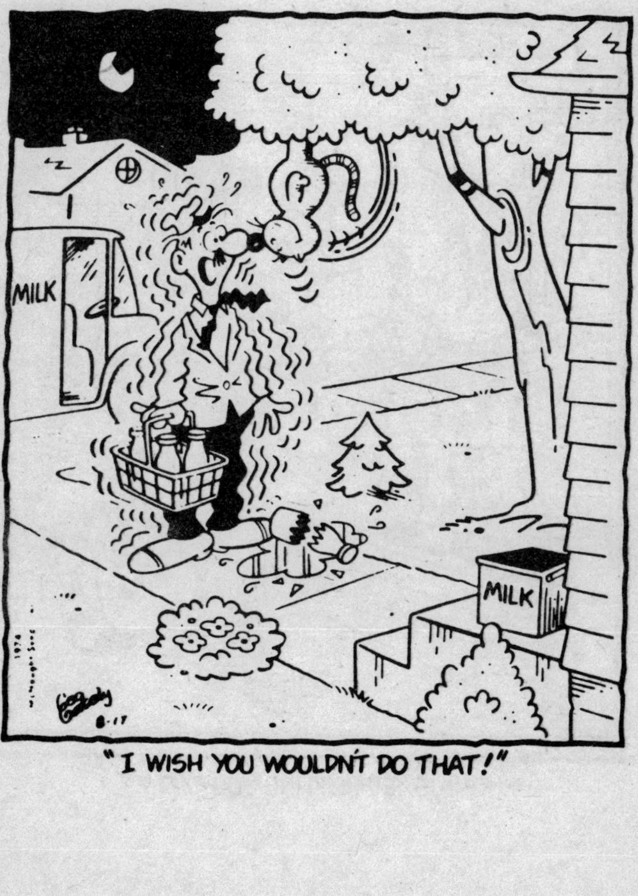
MILK
MILK

"I WISH YOU WOULDN'T DO THAT!"

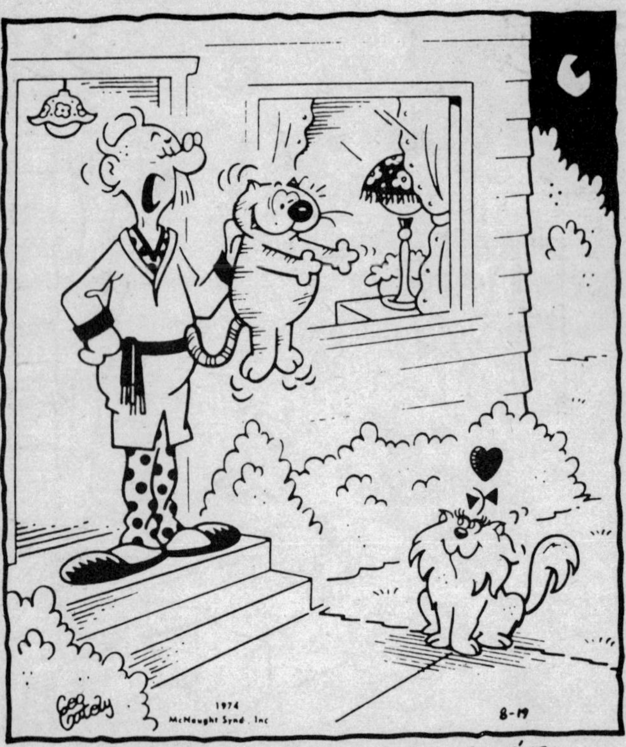
1974
McNaught Synd., Inc
8-19

"PLEASE HOLD THE ROMANCE UNTIL I'VE FINISHED PUTTING YOU OUT!"

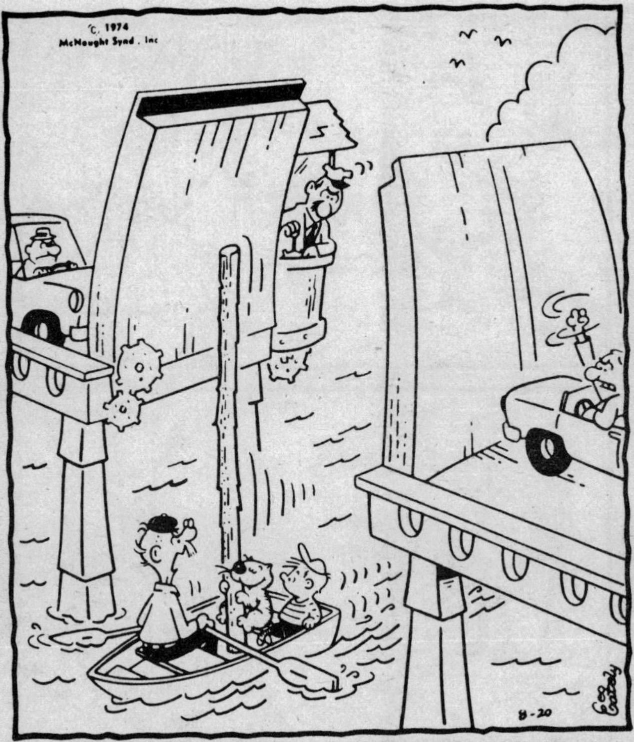
©, 1974
McNaught Synd. Inc
8-20
Geo Gately

"WHY DOES HEATHCLIFF ALWAYS BRING THAT STUPID SCRATCHING POST ?!"

© 1974
McNaught Synd., Inc
8-23
CLICK

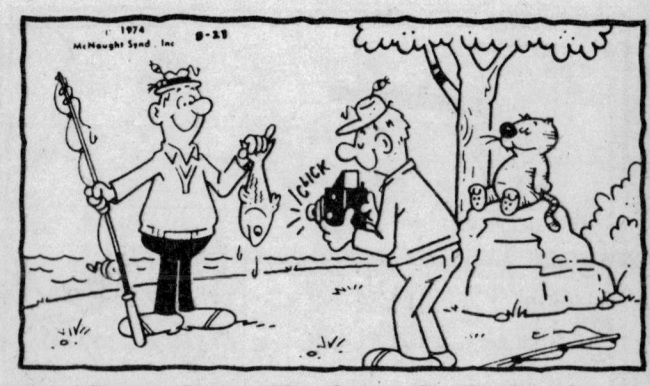

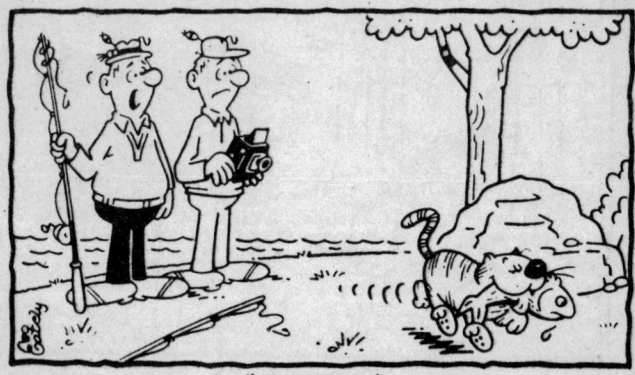

"THANKS."

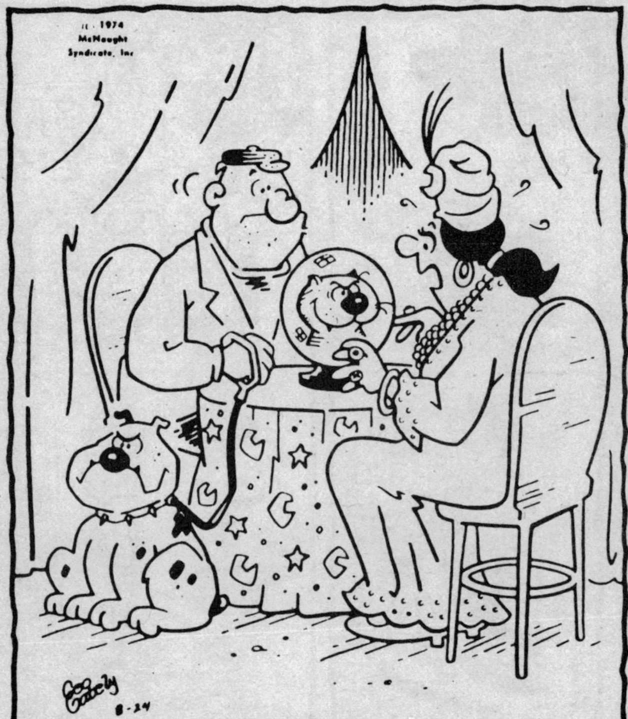
© 1974
McNaught
Syndicate, Inc
8-24

"I SEE BIG TROUBLE AHEAD FOR SOMEONE CLOSE TO YOU ... YOUR DOG!!"

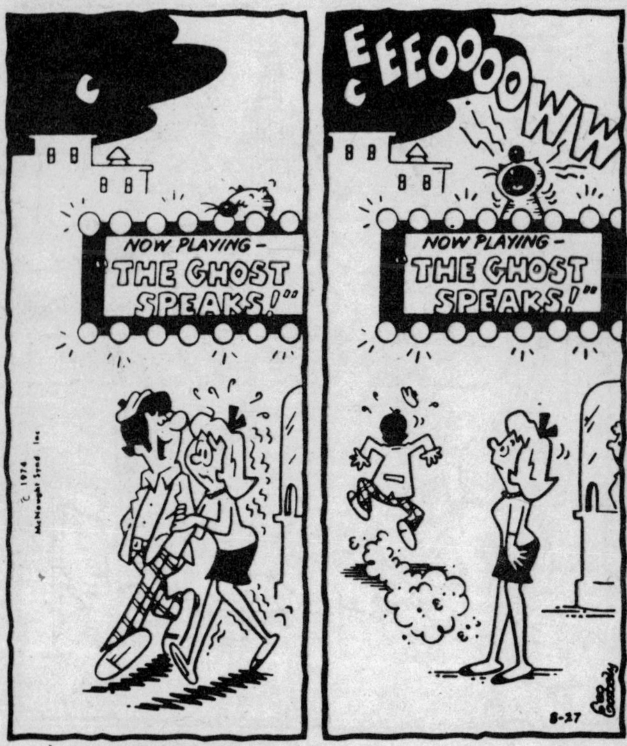
NOW PLAYING -
"THE GHOST SPEAKS!"
EEEOOOOOWW
NOW PLAYING -
"THE GHOST SPEAKS!"
8-27

"OH, COME NOW, ALICE...
IT WAS ONLY A MOVIE."

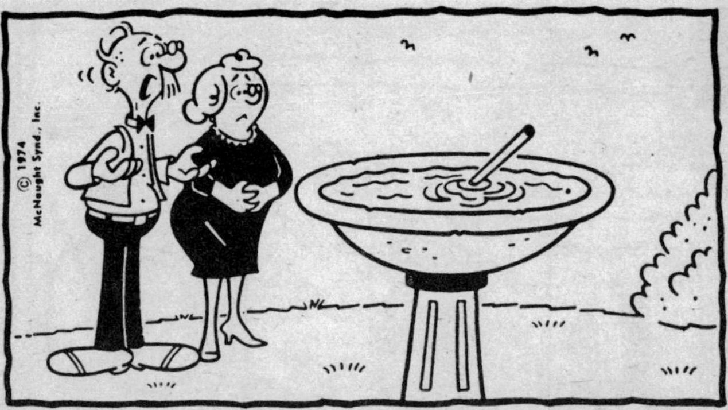
© 1974
McNaught Synd., Inc.

"HOW COME WE NEVER SEE ANY BIRDS IN OUR BIRDBATH?"

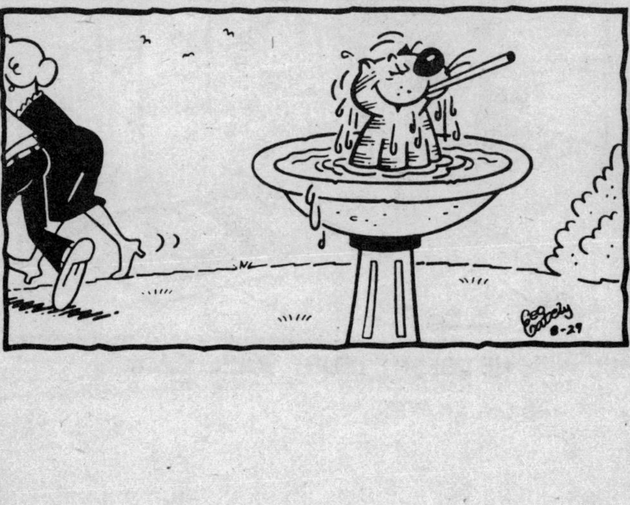
8-29

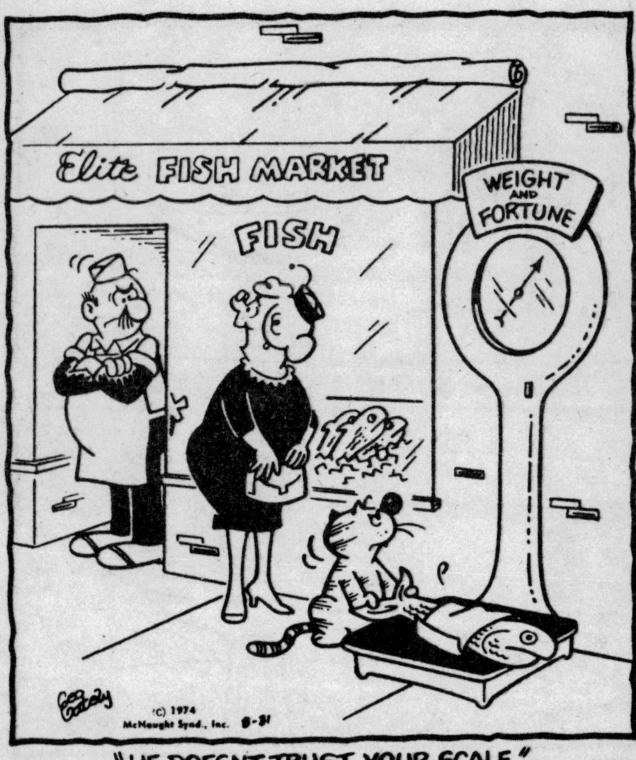
Elite FISH MARKET
FISH
WEIGHT AND FORTUNE
Geo Gately
(C) 1974
McNaught Synd., Inc. 8-31

"HE DOESN'T TRUST YOUR SCALE."

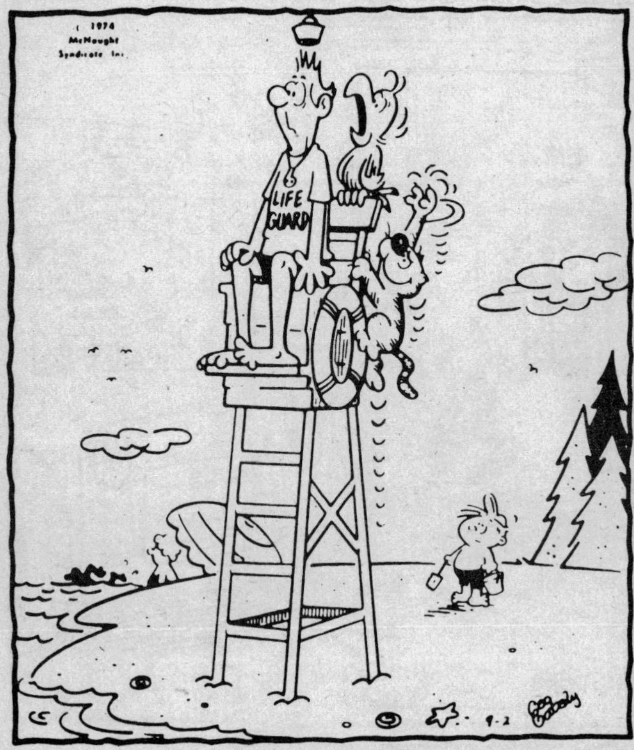
© 1974 McNaught Syndicate Inc.
LIFE GUARD
9-2

"HELP!"

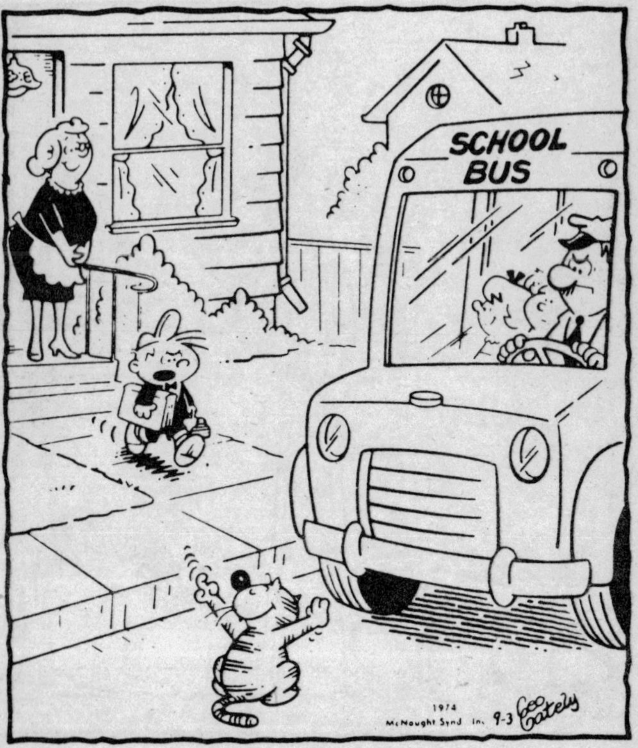
SCHOOL
BUS
1974
McNaught Synd Inc 9-3 Geo Gately

"QUIT RUBBING IT IN!"

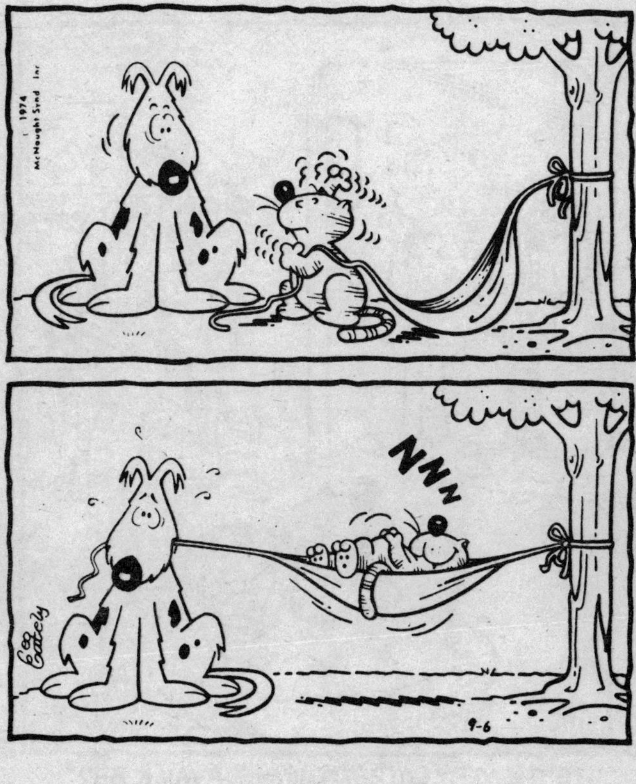
© 1974 McNaught Synd Inc
NNN
Gately
9-6

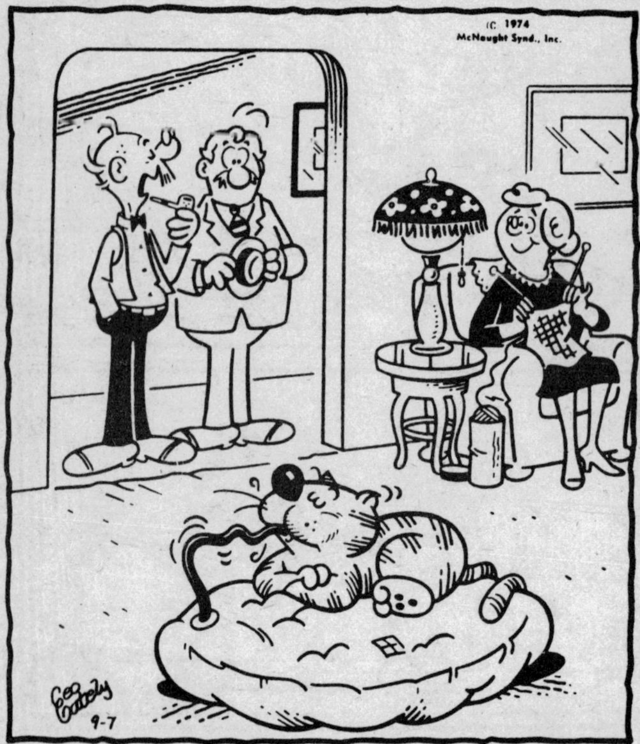
(C 1974
McNaught Synd., Inc.
Geo Crately
9-7

"IT'S THE VERY LATEST THING... A MILK BED."

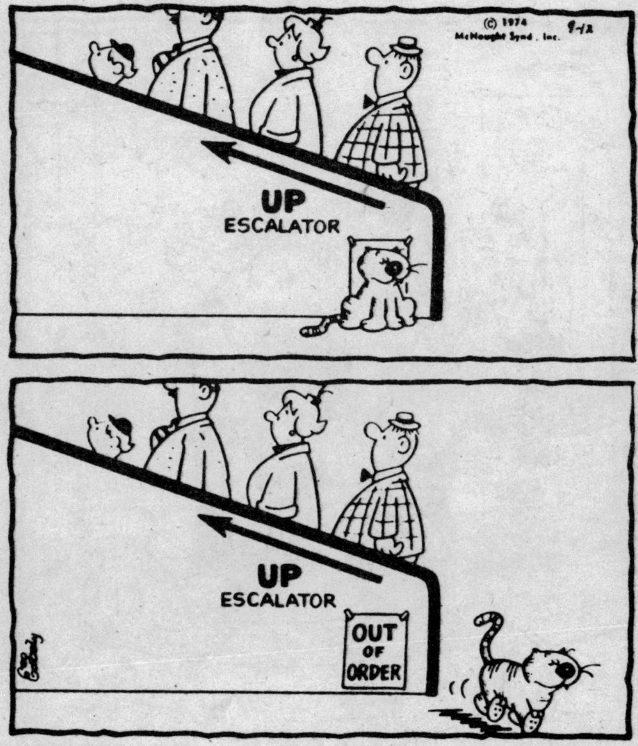

© 1974 McNaught Synd., Inc.
9-12
UP
ESCALATOR
UP
ESCALATOR
OUT OF ORDER

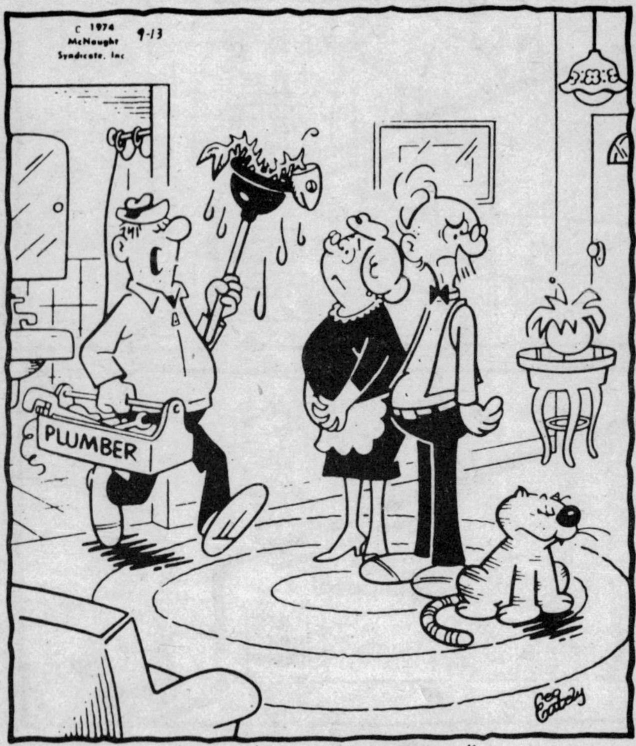
c 1974
McNaught
Syndicate, Inc
9-13
PLUMBER

"HERE'S YOUR TROUBLE."

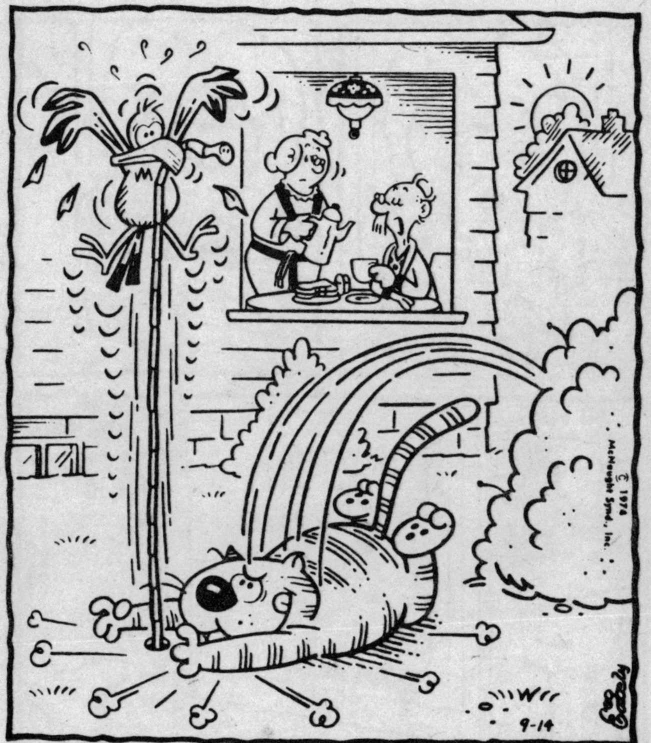
© 1978 McNaught Synd., Inc.
9-14

"THE EARLY BIRD CATCHES HEATHCLIFF!"

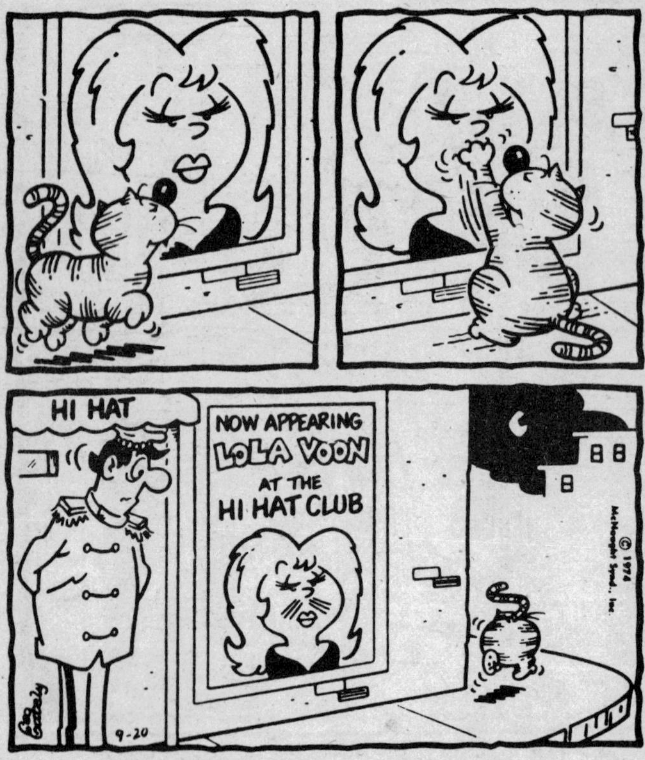
HI HAT
NOW APPEARING
LOLA VOON
AT THE
HI HAT CLUB
© 1974 McNaught Synd., Inc.
9-20

"GET OUT THERE AND CHASE THAT CAT OUT OF OUR YARD!"

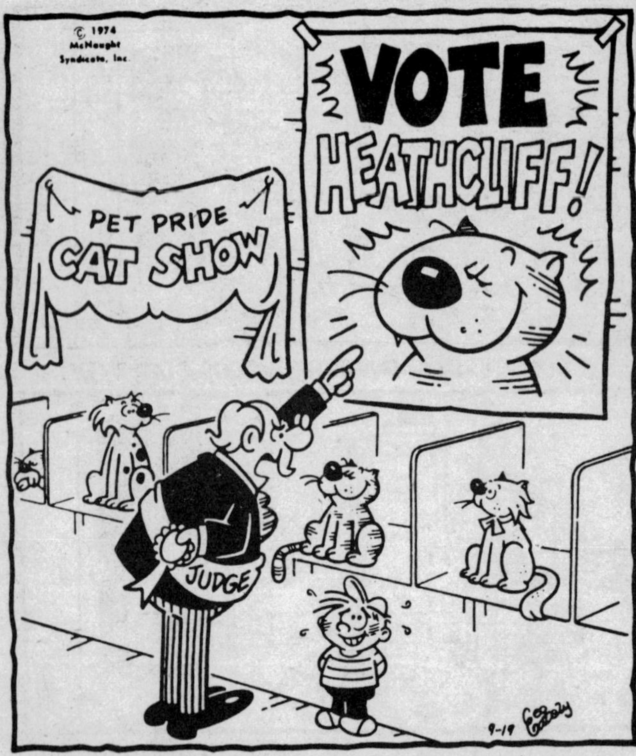
© 1974
McNaught
Syndicate, Inc.
VOTE
HEATHCLIFF!
PET PRIDE
CAT SHOW
JUDGE
9-19

"*THAT* IS AGAINST THE RULES!"

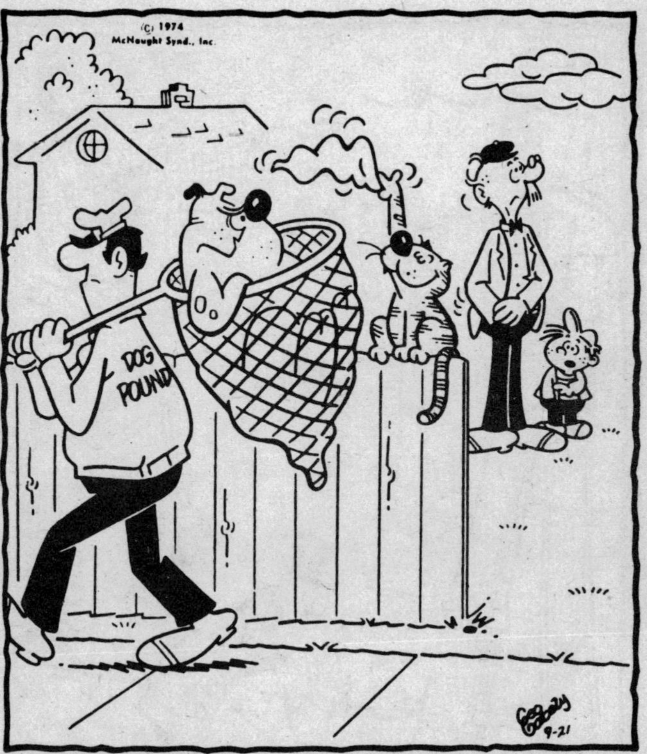

(C) 1974
McNaught Synd., Inc.
DOG POUND
9-21

"YOUR HANDKERCHIEF?... I THINK HEATHCLIFF HAS IT."

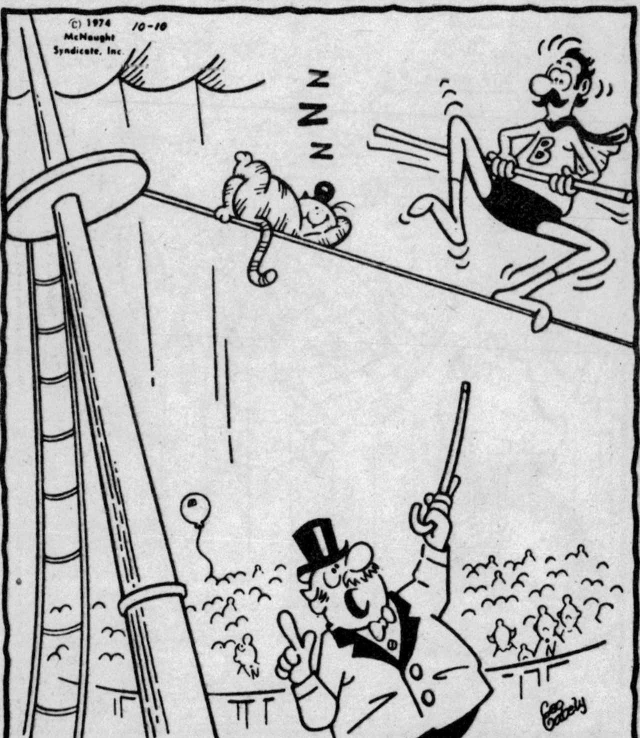

© 1974 McNaught Syndicate, Inc.
10-10
Z Z Z
B

"FOR HIS NEXT DEATH DEFYING FEAT,
THE GREAT BOLDINI WILL..."

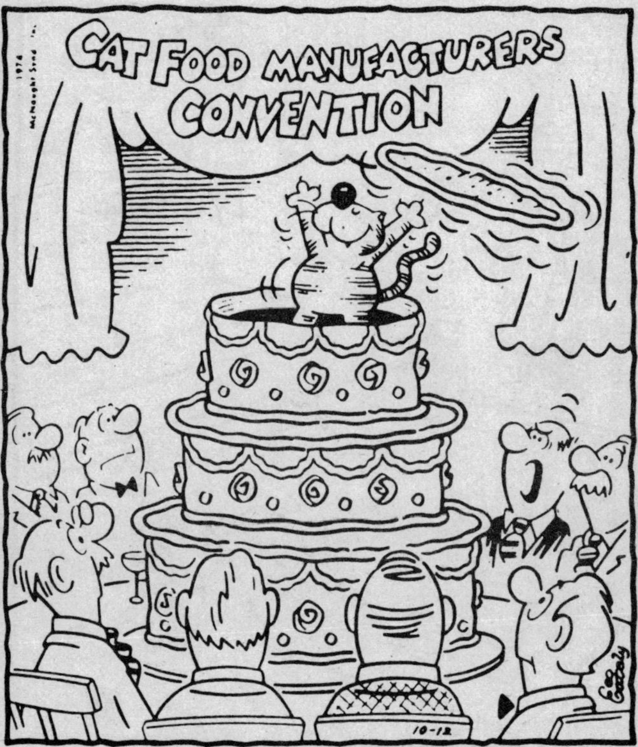
CAT FOOD MANUFACTURERS
CONVENTION
10-12

"I WAS EXPECTING A BLONDE!"

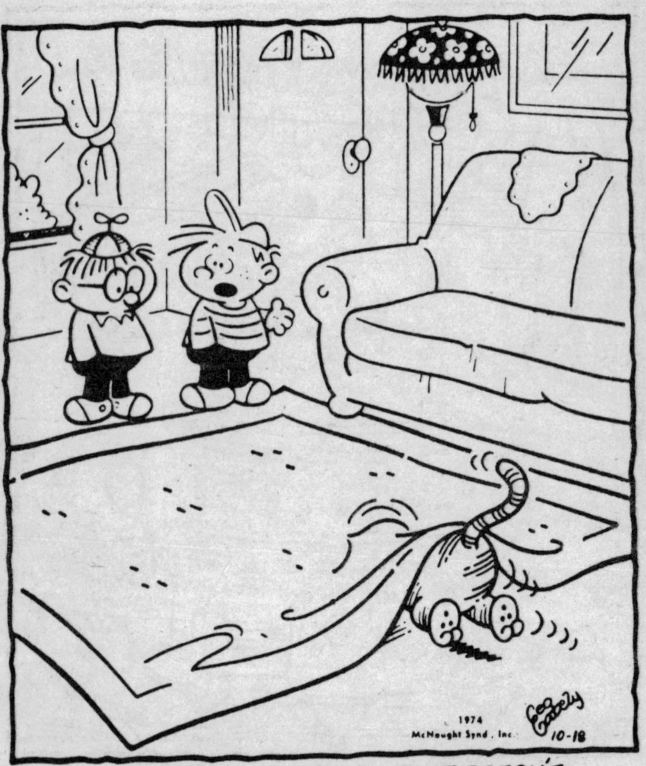
1974
McNaught Synd., Inc.
10-18

"IN THIS HOUSE, EVEN AN *ANT* DOESN'T STAND A CHANCE OF SURVIVAL!"

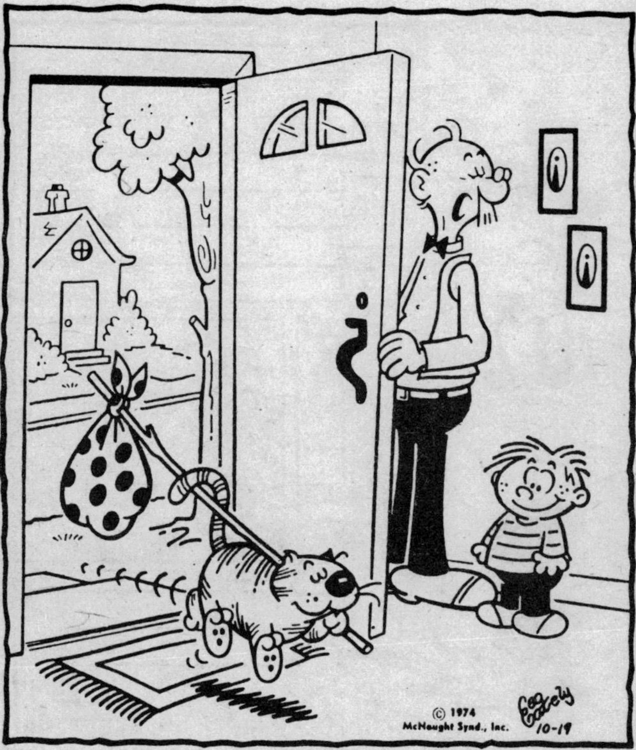
© 1974
McNaught Synd., Inc.
10-19

"HE'S GIVING US ANOTHER CHANCE."

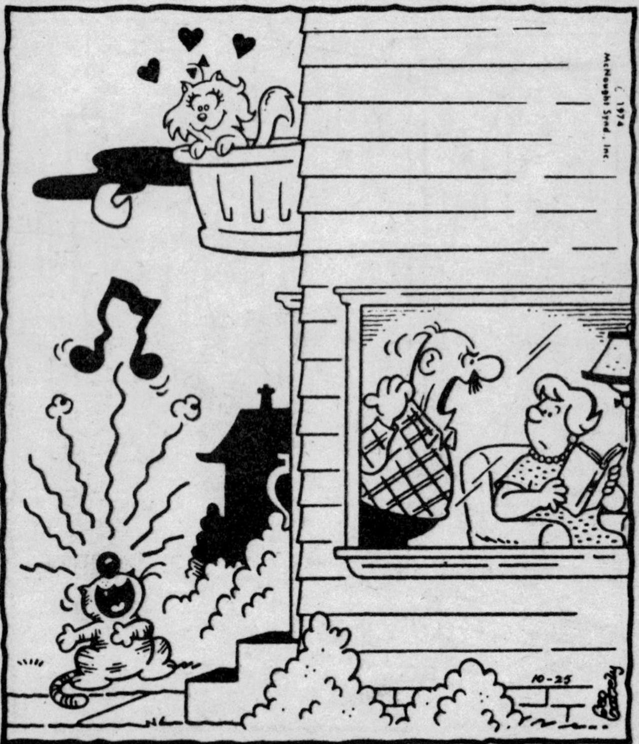
© 1974 McNaught Synd., Inc.
10-25

"WE'VE GOTTA TEAR DOWN THAT BALCONY!"

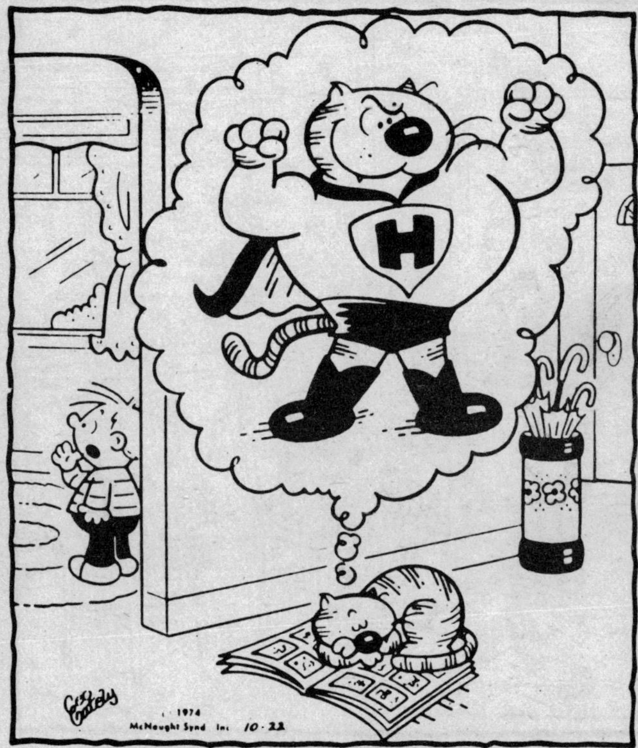
H
1974
McNaught Synd Inc 10-22

"GRANDMA, HAVE YOU SEEN MY COMIC BOOK?"

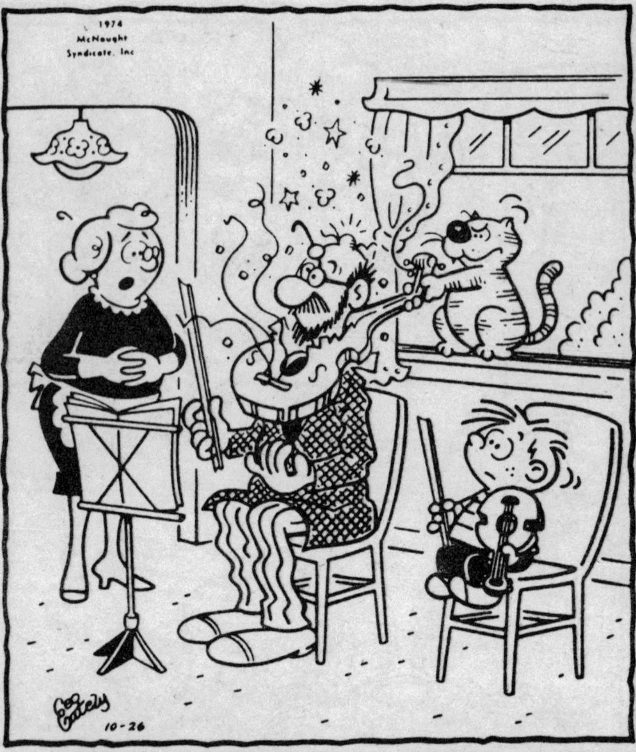

1974
McNaught
Syndicate, Inc
10-26

"I SHOULD HAVE WARNED YOU, PROFESSOR...NEVER MENTION 'CAT GUT' IN FRONT OF HEATHCLIFF!"

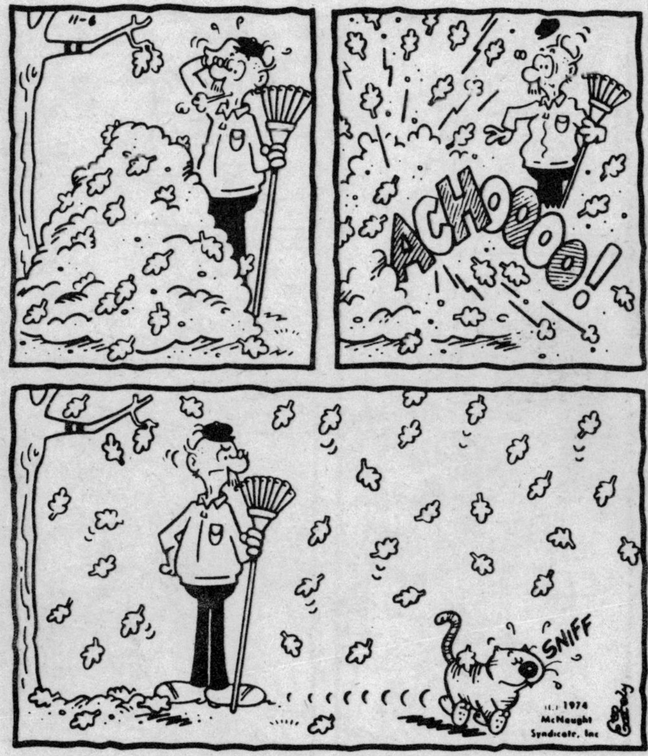
11-6
ACHOOOO!
SNIFF
11-6 1974
McNaught
Syndicate, Inc

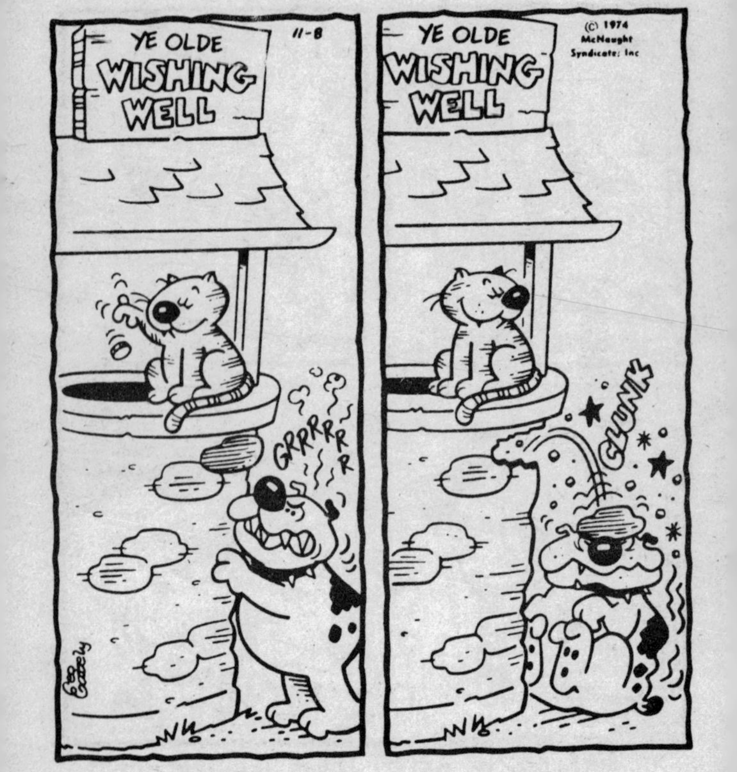
YE OLDE WISHING WELL
11-8
GRRRRRR
YE OLDE WISHING WELL
(C) 1974 McNaught Syndicate, Inc
GLUNK

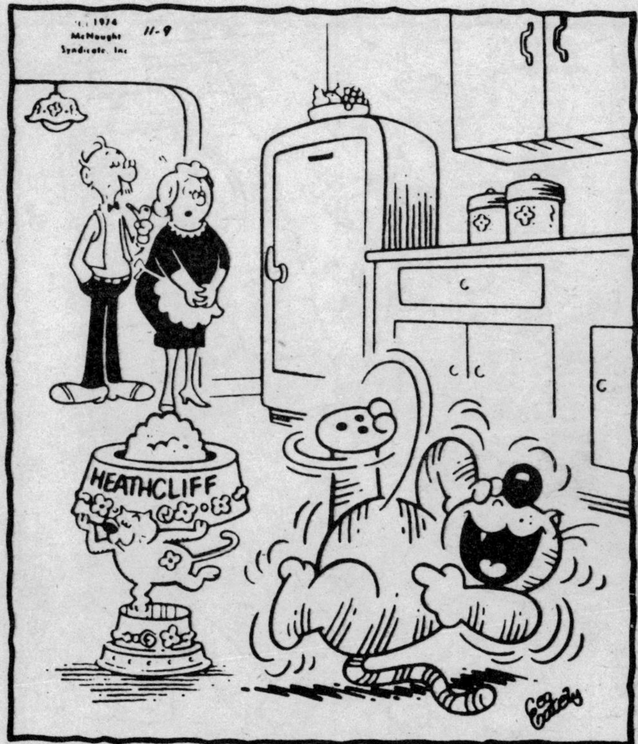
© 1974
McNaught
Syndicate, Inc
11-9
HEATHCLIFF

"I'M AFRAID HE DOESN'T THINK MUCH OF HIS NEW BOWL!"

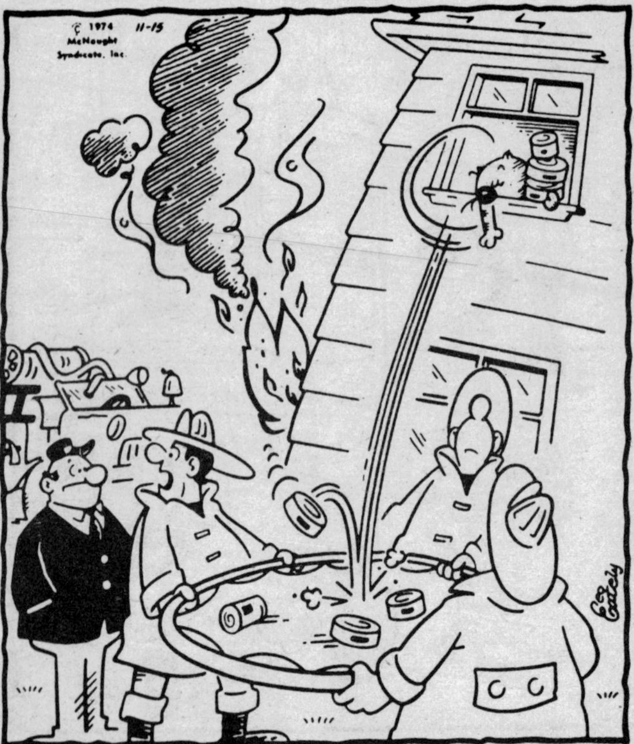
© 1974 McNaught Syndicate, Inc.
11-15
Geo Crosby

"SO FAR, ALL WE'RE GETTING IS CANS OF CAT FOOD!"

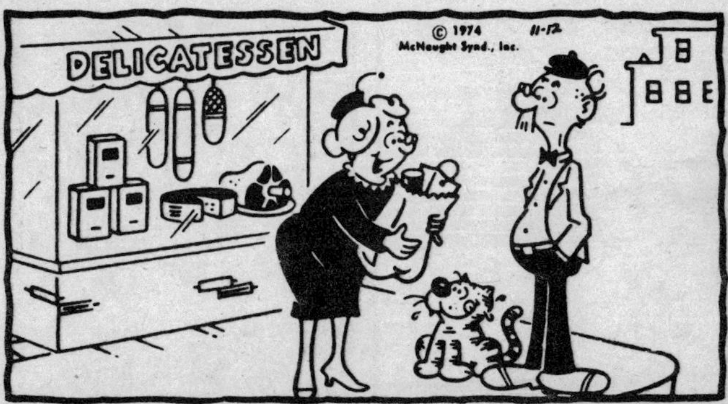

DELICATESSEN
© 1974 11-12
McNaught Synd., Inc.

"I BOUGHT FRESH SALMON, ANCHOVIES, SHRIMP SALAD, CHICKEN LIVERS, MARINATED HERRING, A CAN OF CAVIAR...

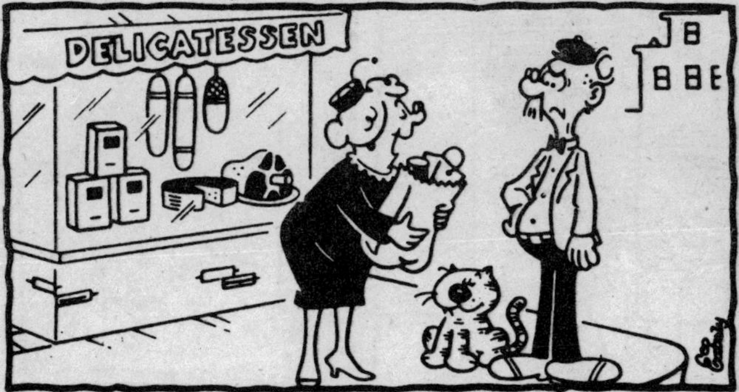

DELICATESSEN

...AND A HALF A POUND OF BALONEY FOR YOU, DEAR."

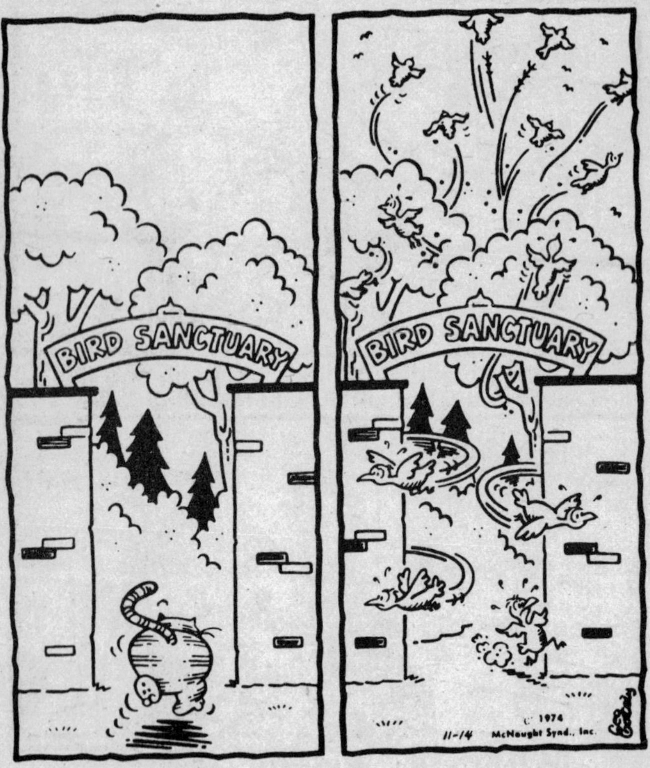
BIRD SANCTUARY
BIRD SANCTUARY
© 1974
11-14 McNaught Synd., Inc.

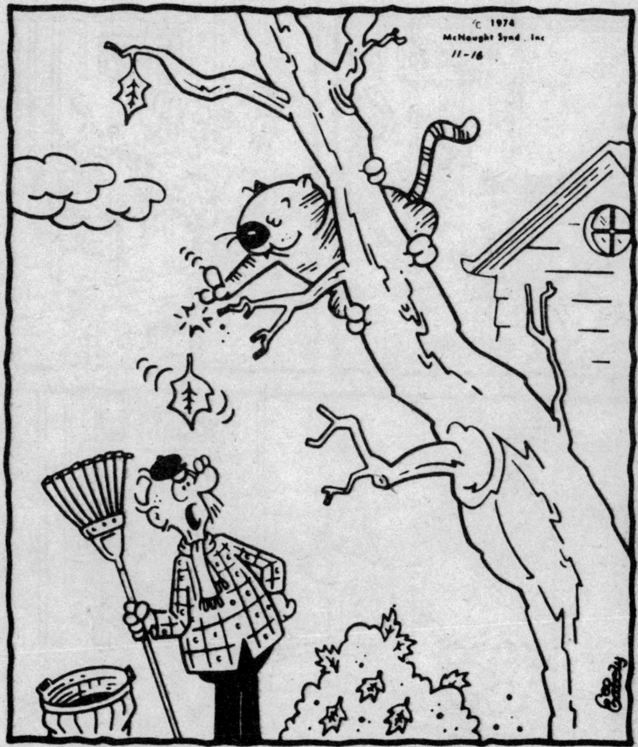
©1974
McNaught Synd., Inc
11-16

"YOU DON'T HAVE TO GET ME EVERY LAST LEAF!"

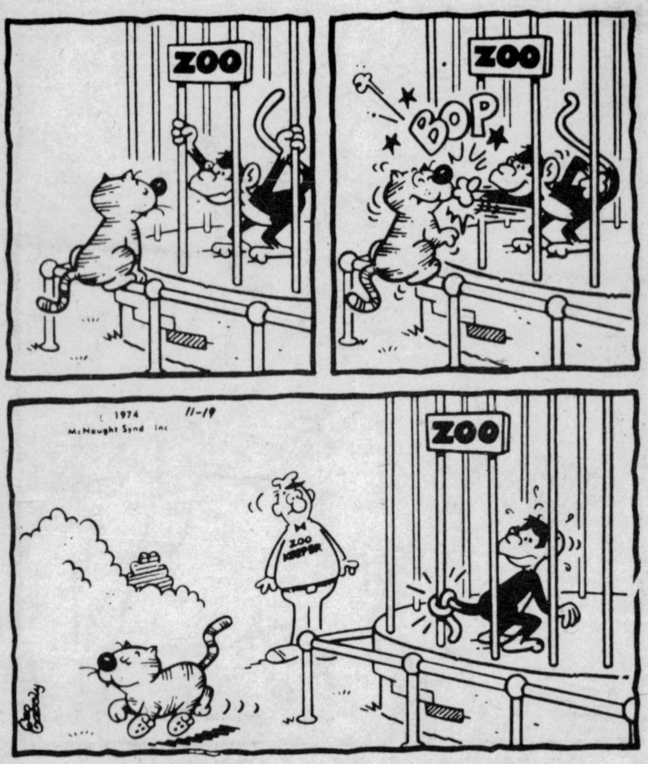
ZOO
ZOO
BOP
© 1974 McNaught Synd Inc
11-19
ZOO
ZOO KEEPER

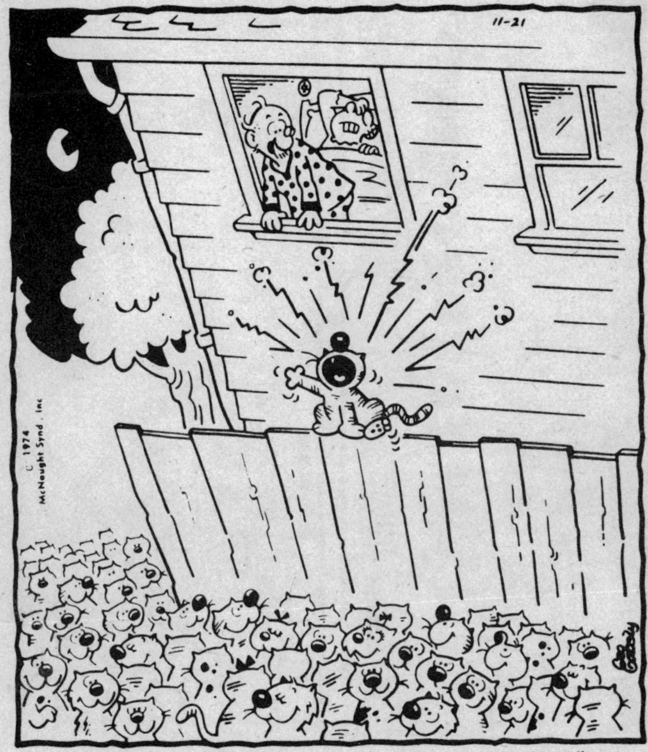
11-21
© 1974 McNaught Synd., Inc

" TONIGHT, HE'S CONDUCTING A ROCK FESTIVAL ! "

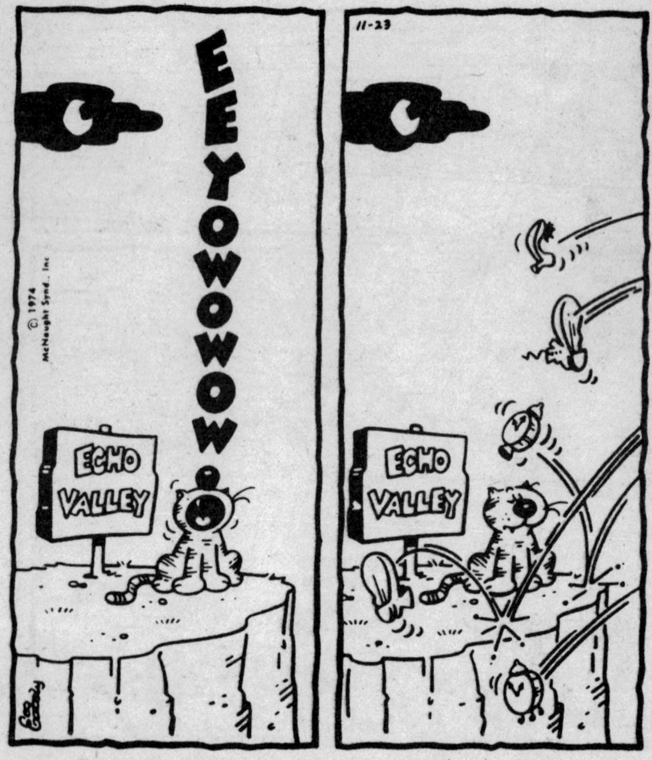

EEYOWOWOWOW
ECHO VALLEY
© 1974 McNaught Synd., Inc
11-23
ECHO VALLEY

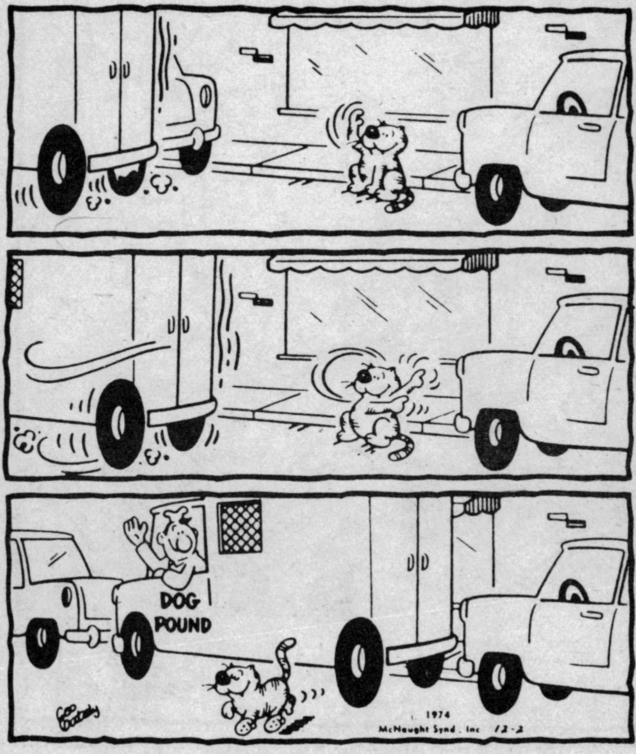
DOG POUND
1974
McNaught Synd., Inc 12-2

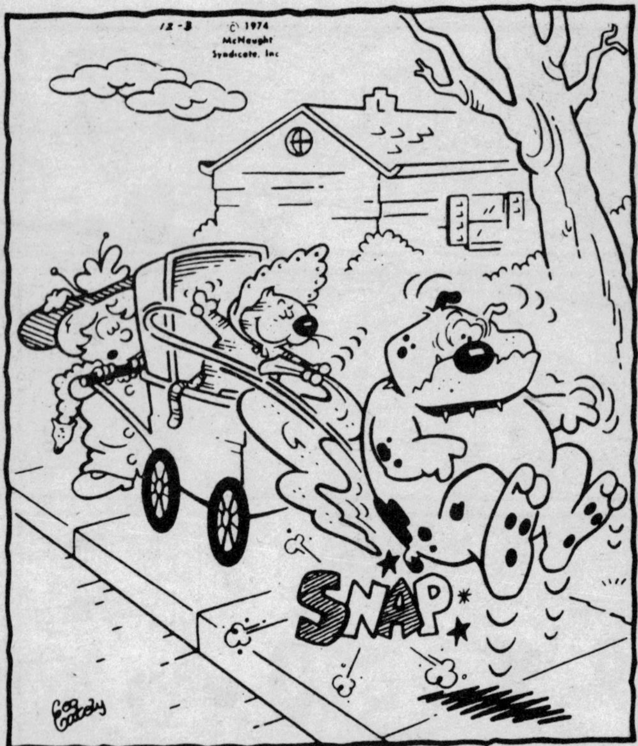
12-3 © 1974 McNaught Syndicate, Inc
SNAP

"STAY UNDER YOUR BLANKET, DEAR... IT'S CHILLY."

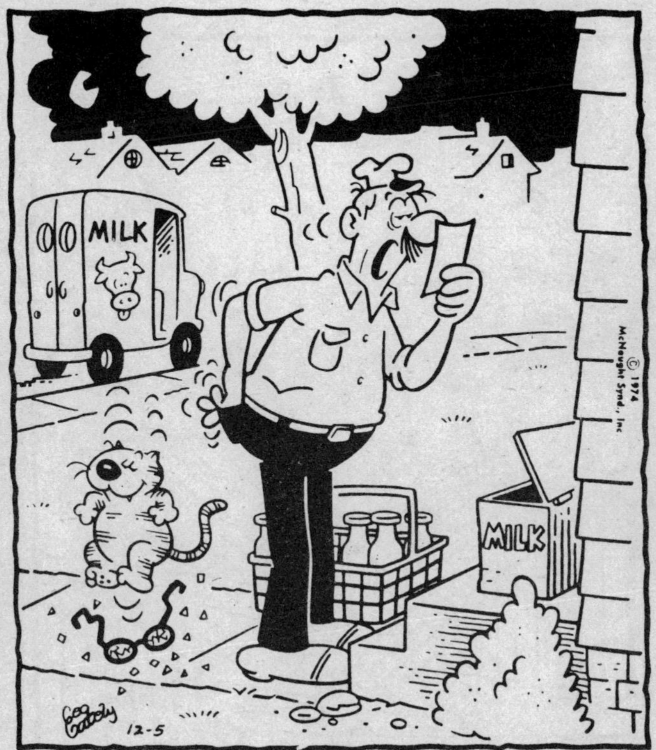
MILK
MILK
© 1974 McNaught Synd., Inc
12-5

"HMMM... DOES THAT SAY 8 QUARTS OR 3 QUARTS? ....WHERE ARE MY GLASSES?"

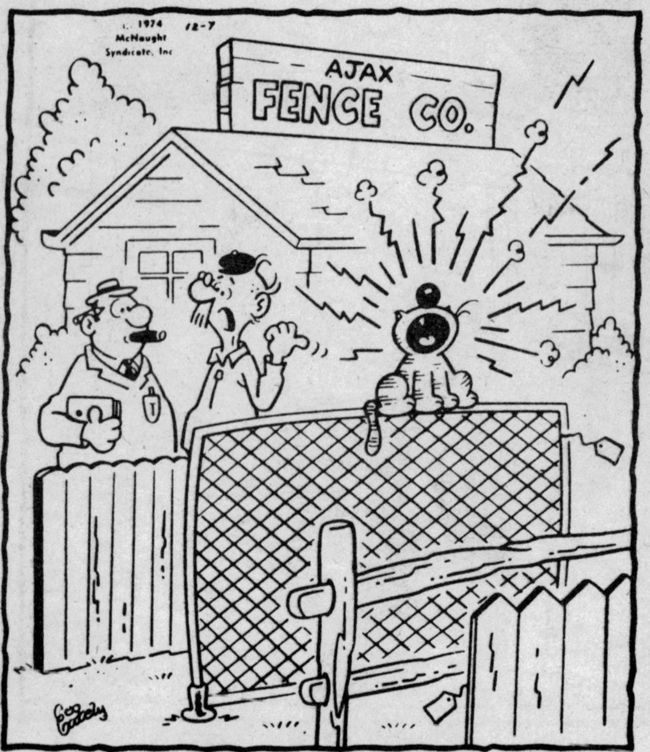
© 1974
McNaught
Syndicate, Inc
12-7
AJAX
FENCE CO.

"I'D LIKE TO PURCHASE SOME NEW FENCING...
BUT HE HAS TO TRY IT OUT FIRST."

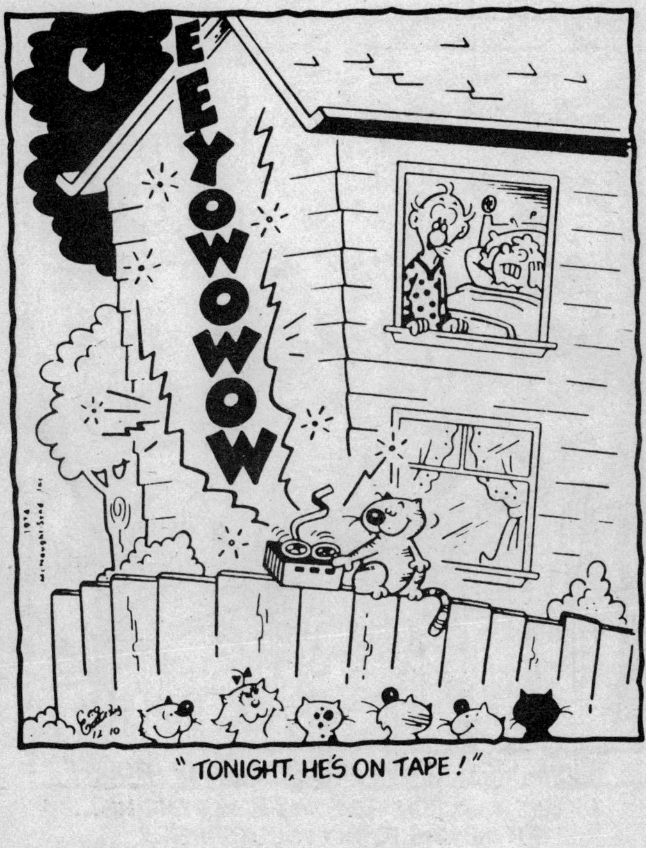
EEEYOWOWOWOW
1974 McNaught Synd. Inc.

" TONIGHT, HE'S ON TAPE ! "

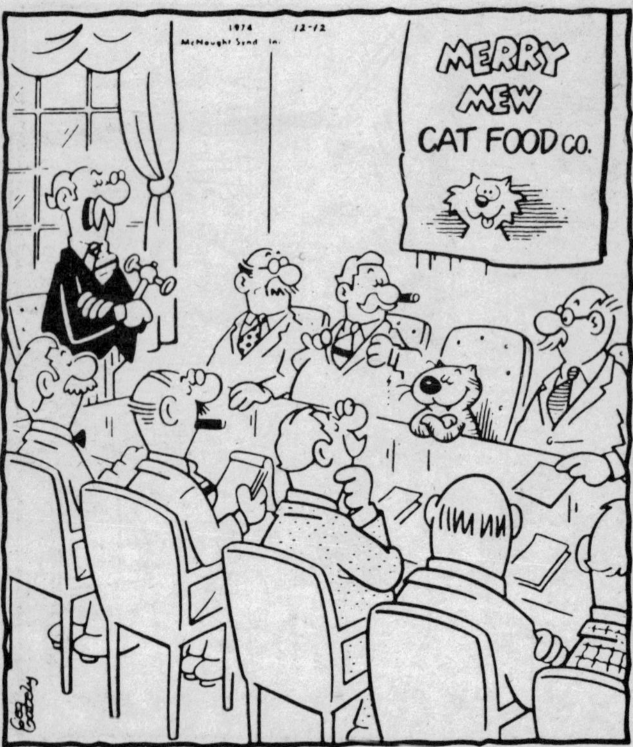
1974 McNaught Synd., Inc.
12-12
MERRY
MEW
CAT FOOD CO.

"SOMEONE LEFT HIM A HUGE BLOCK OF STOCK."

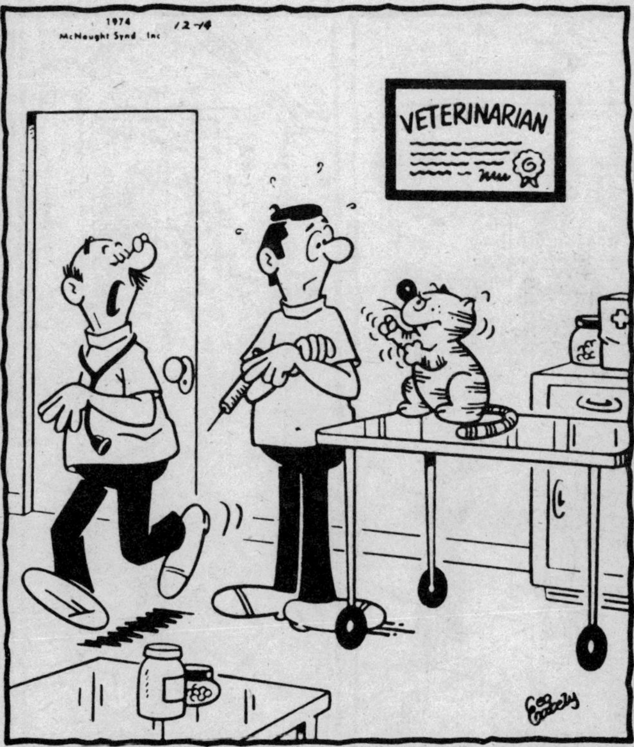
1974
McNaught Synd Inc
12-14
VETERINARIAN

"HE'S BEEN HERE BEFORE ... YOU GIVE HIM HIS SHOT...
I'LL BE WAITING FOR YOU ON TOP OF THE FILE CABINET!"

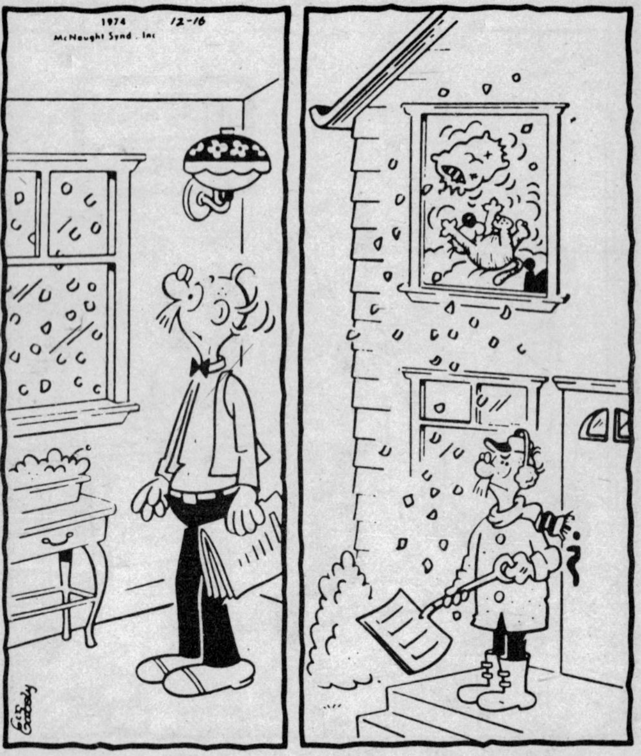
1974 12-16
McNaught Synd. Inc

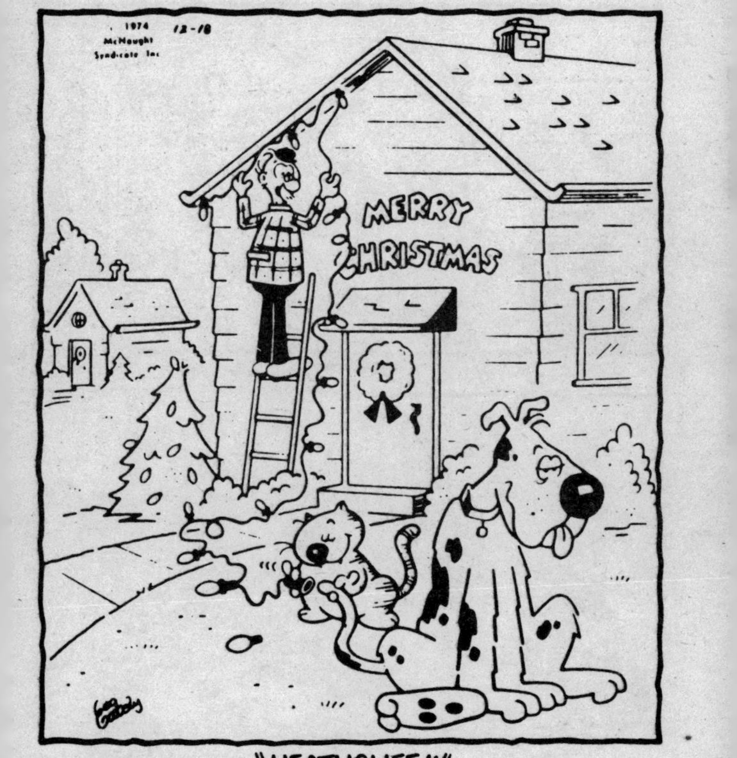
© 1974 McNaught Syndicate Inc
12-18
MERRY
CHRISTMAS

"HEATHCLIFF!!"

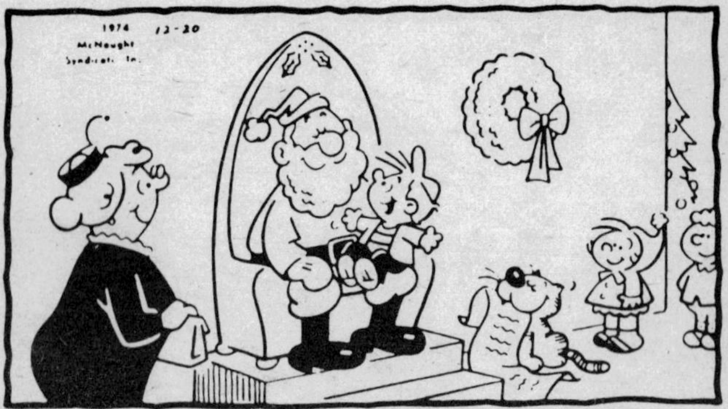
1974 12-20 McNaught Syndicate Inc.

"A SET OF TRAINS, A BASKETBALL, A DUMP TRUCK..."

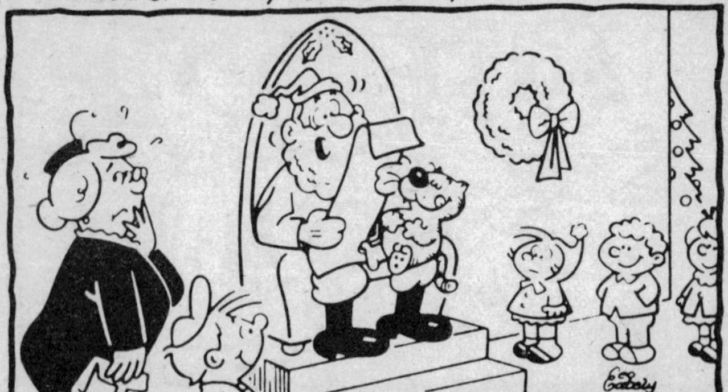

"BROOK TROUT, TUNA, RED SNAPPER, MACKEREL, CARP, STRIPED BASS, CODFISH, HERRING, FLOUNDER, PERCH..."

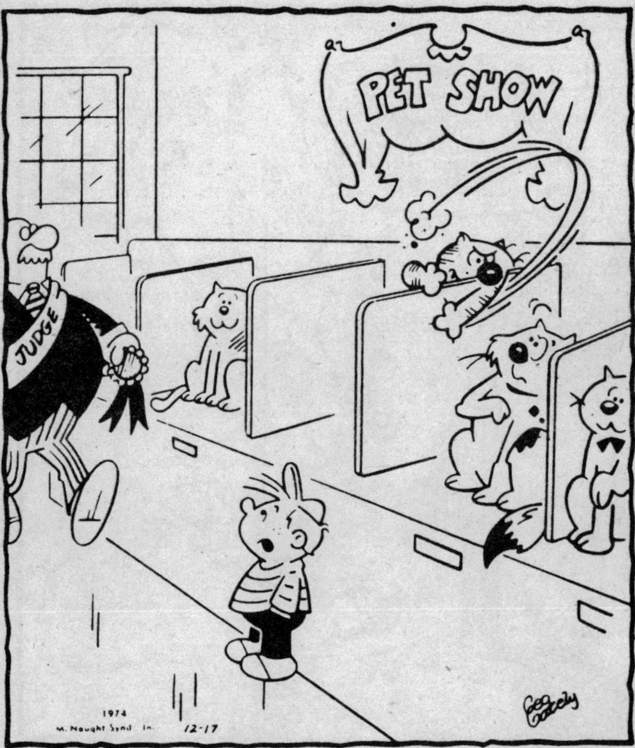
PET SHOW
JUDGE
1974
M. Naught Synd. Inc.
12-17

"COOL IT, HEATHCLIFF!... HERE COME TH' JUDGE!"

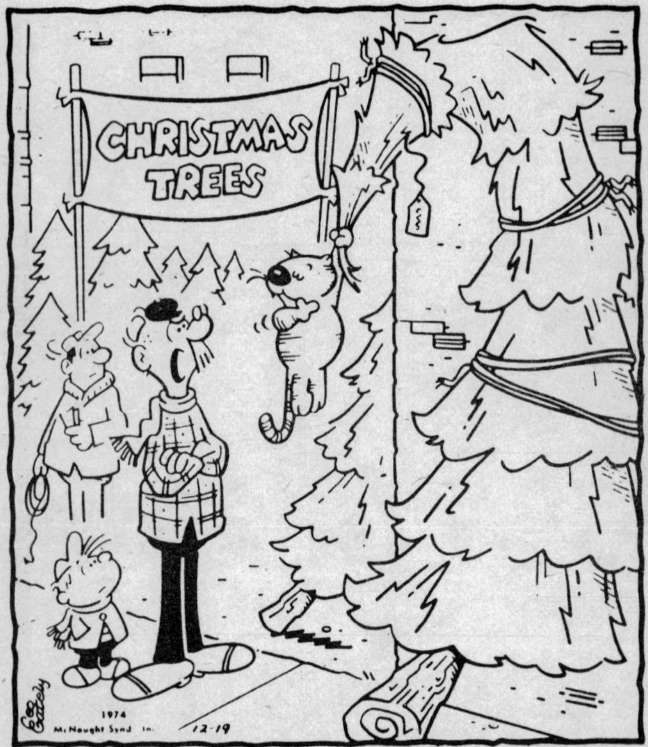
CHRISTMAS TREES
1974
McNaught Synd Inc
12-19

"I'LL PICK OUT THE TREE, IF YOU DON'T MIND!"

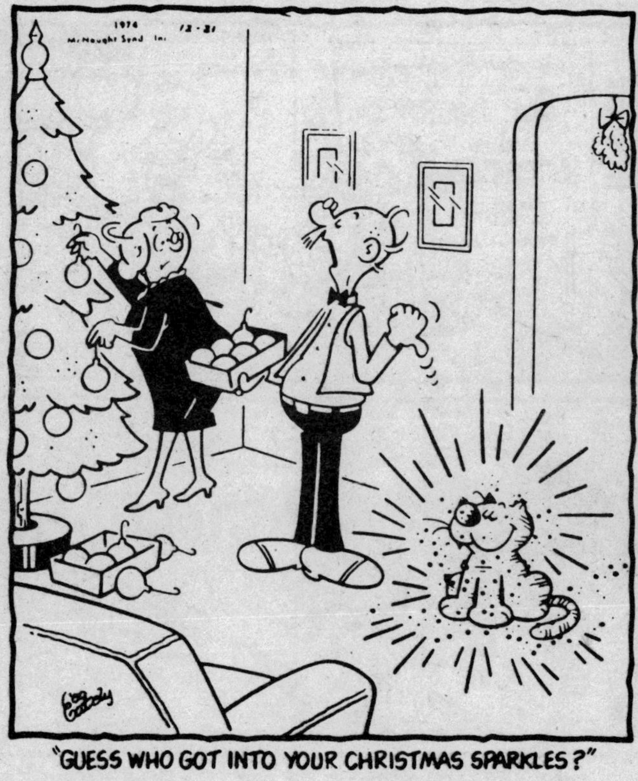
1974
McNaught Synd Inc
12-31

"GUESS WHO GOT INTO YOUR CHRISTMAS SPARKLES?"

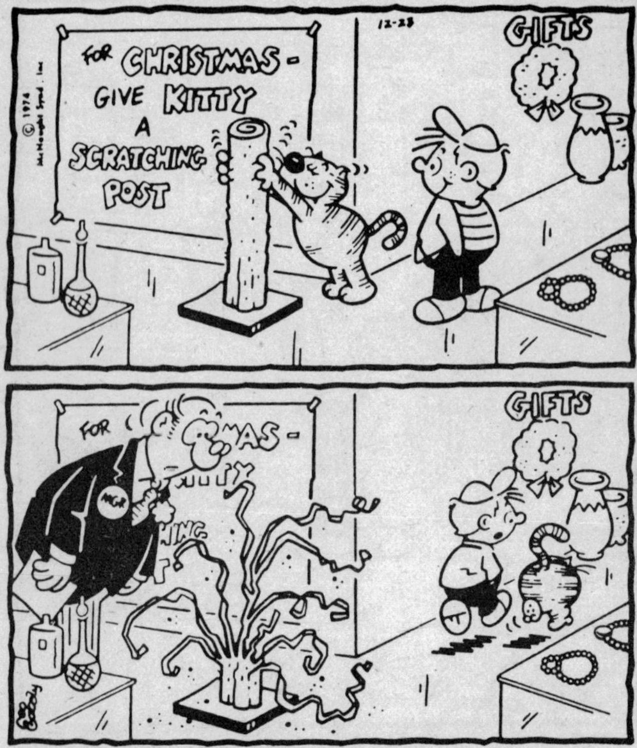
12-23
FOR CHRISTMAS -
GIVE KITTY
A
SCRATCHING
POST
GIFTS
© 1974 McNaught Synd., Inc.
GIFTS
MGR

"THEY JUST DON'T MAKE 'EM THE WAY THEY USED TO!"

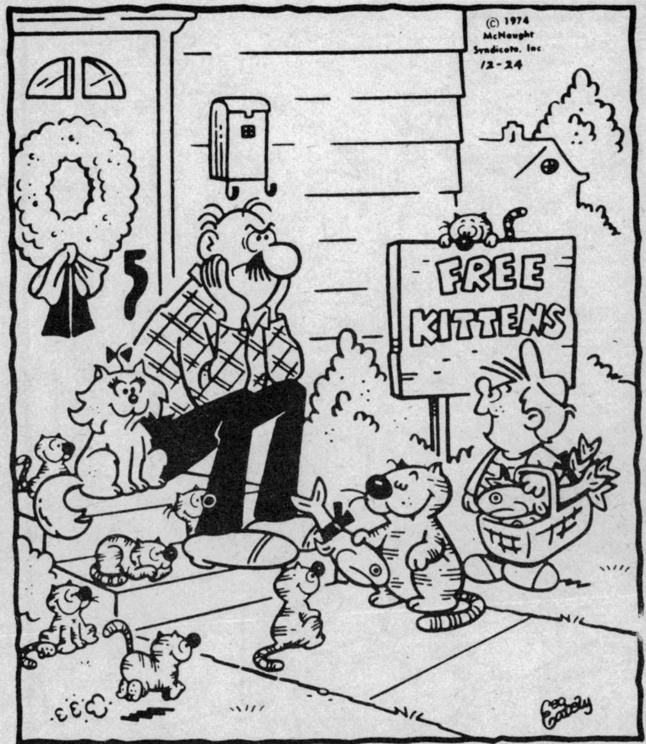
© 1974
McNaught
Syndicate, Inc
12-24
5
FREE
KITTENS

"HEATHCLIFF WANTS TO MAKE SURE THAT EACH LITTLE ONE RECEIVES A CHRISTMAS PRESENT."

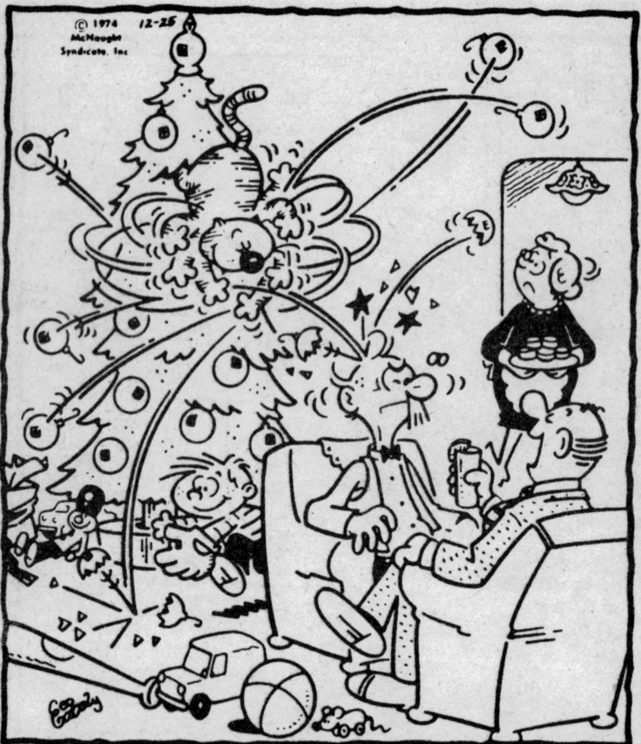
© 1974 McNaught Syndicate, Inc
12-26

"HEATHCLIFF CERTAINLY ENJOYS THE CHRISTMAS TREE."

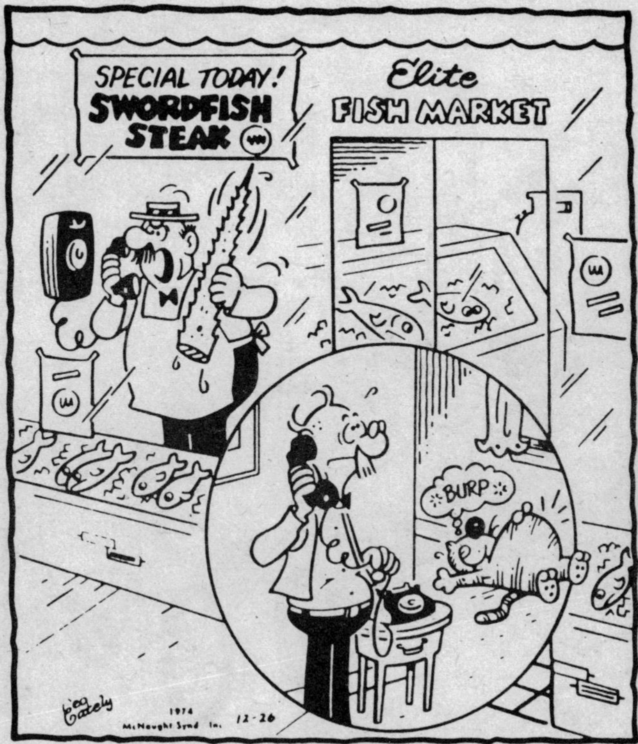
SPECIAL TODAY!
SWORDFISH STEAK
Elite
FISH MARKET
BURP
1974
McNaught Synd Inc.
12-26

"MR. NUTMEG... HEATHCLIFF WAS IN HERE.... GUESS WHAT HE DID TO TODAY'S SPECIAL?!"

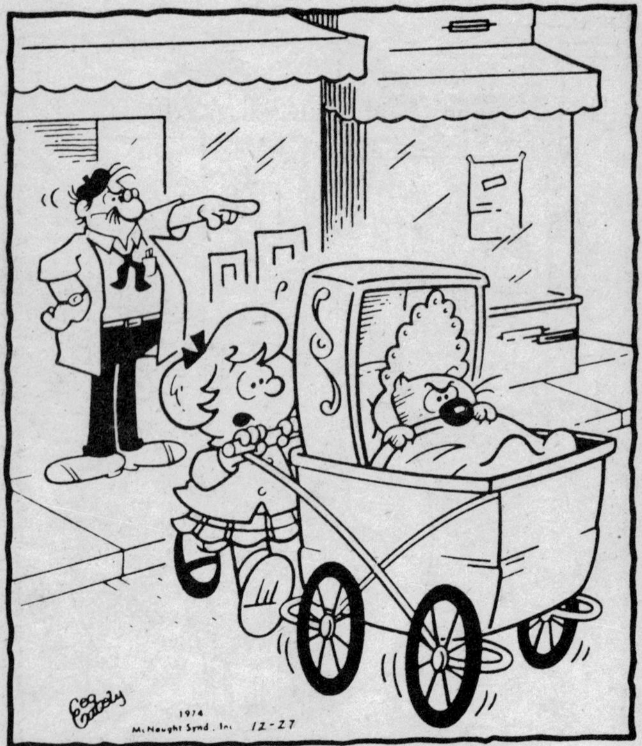
1974
McNaught Synd. Inc 12-27

"MY!... HE CERTAINLY IS A GROUCHY BABY PHOTOGRAPHER!"

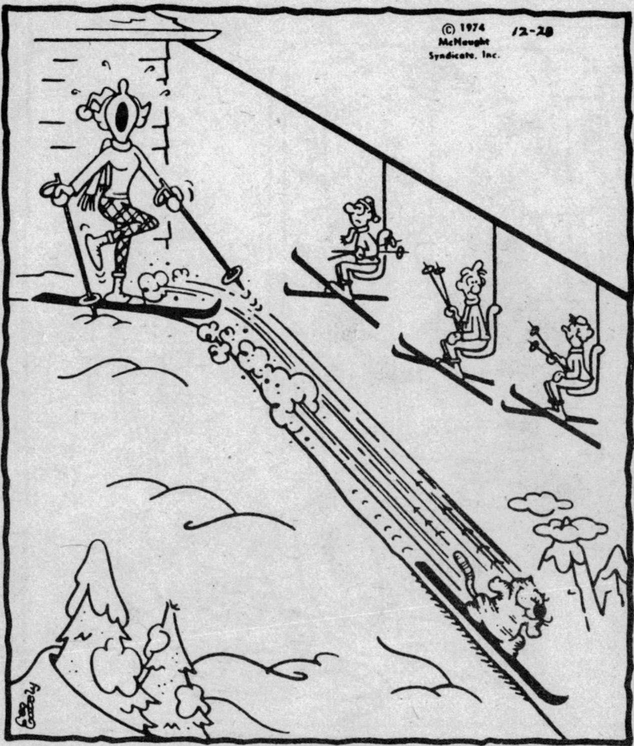
© 1974
McNaught
Syndicate, Inc.
12-28

"STOP THIEF!"

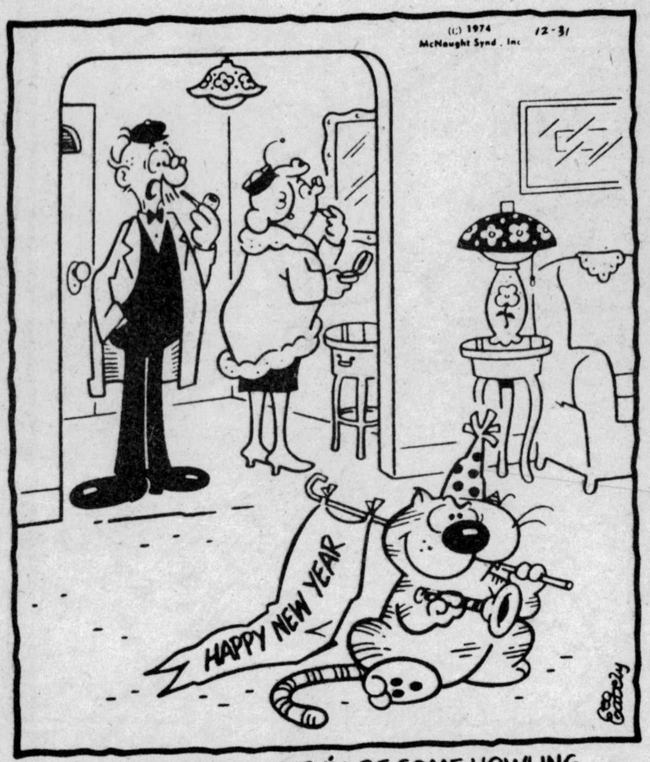
(C) 1974
McNaught Synd. Inc
12-31
HAPPY NEW YEAR

"OH, BROTHER!... THEY'LL BE SOME HOWLING ON THE BACK FENCE TONIGHT!"

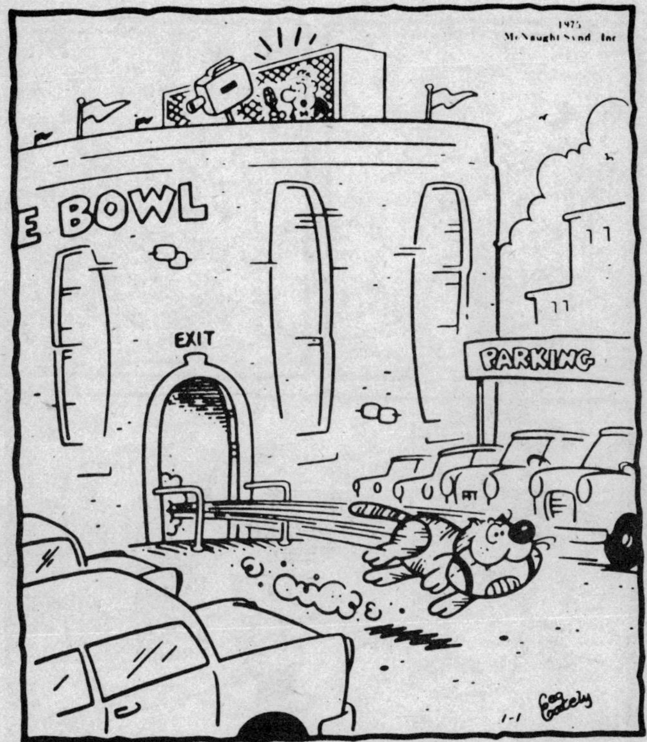
1975
McNaught Synd. Inc
E BOWL
EXIT
PARKING
1-1

"ALL RIGHT, FANS... LET'S HAVE ANOTHER LOOK AT THAT ON INSTANT REPLAY..."

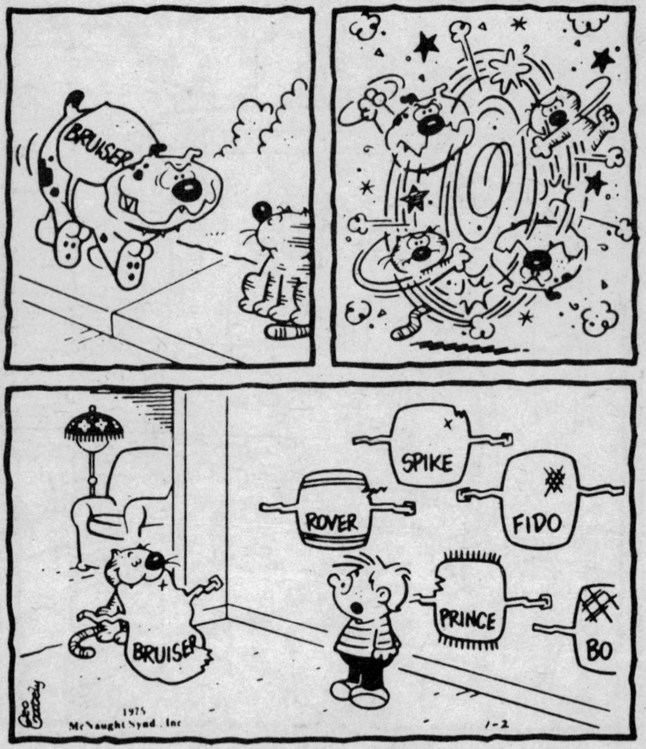
BRUISER
SPIKE
ROVER
FIDO
PRINCE
BO
BRUISER
1975
McNaught Synd., Inc
1-2
"ANOTHER ONE ?!!"

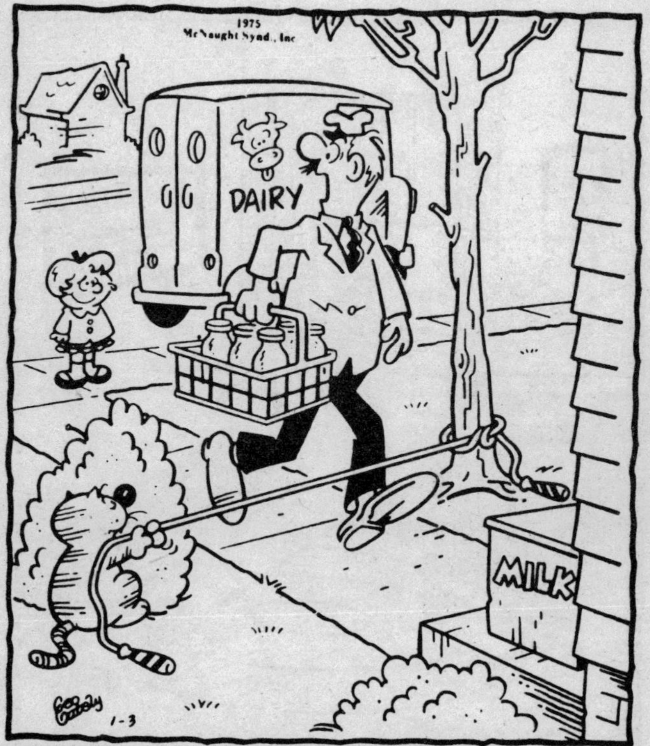
1975
McNaught Synd., Inc
DAIRY
MILK
1-3

"NO, I HAVEN'T SEEN YOUR LOST JUMPROPE...
BUT I'LL KEEP AN EYE OPEN FOR IT."

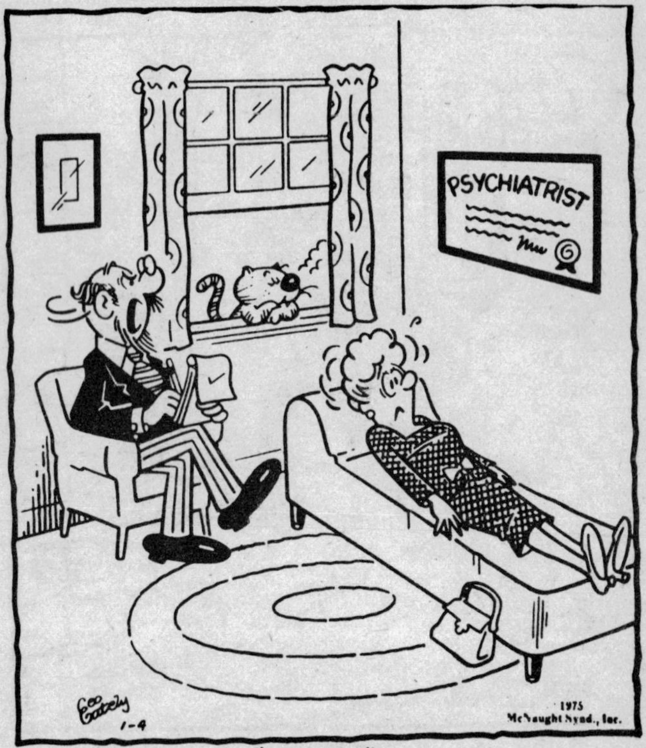
PSYCHIATRIST
1-4
1975
McNaught Synd., Inc.
"SCAT!"

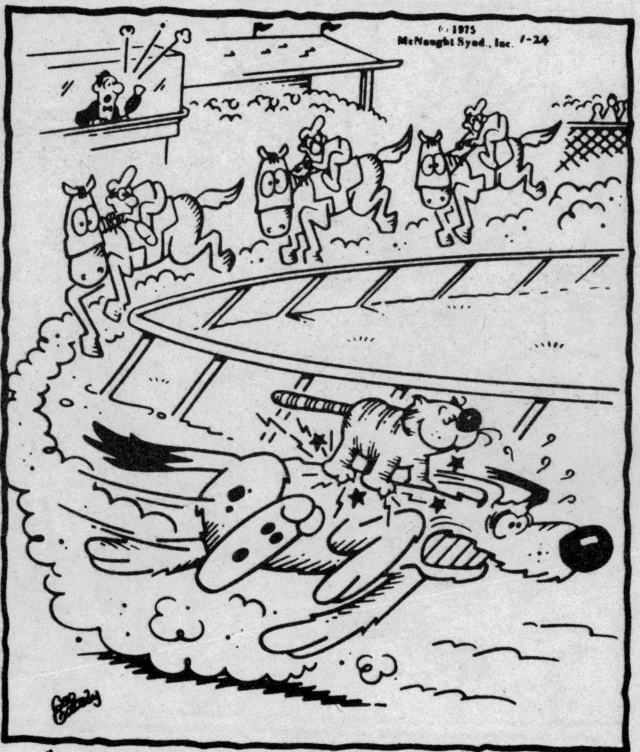
© 1975
McNaught Synd., Inc. 1-24

"...AND LEADING AS THEY HIT THE STRETCH, IT'S...IT'S...!"

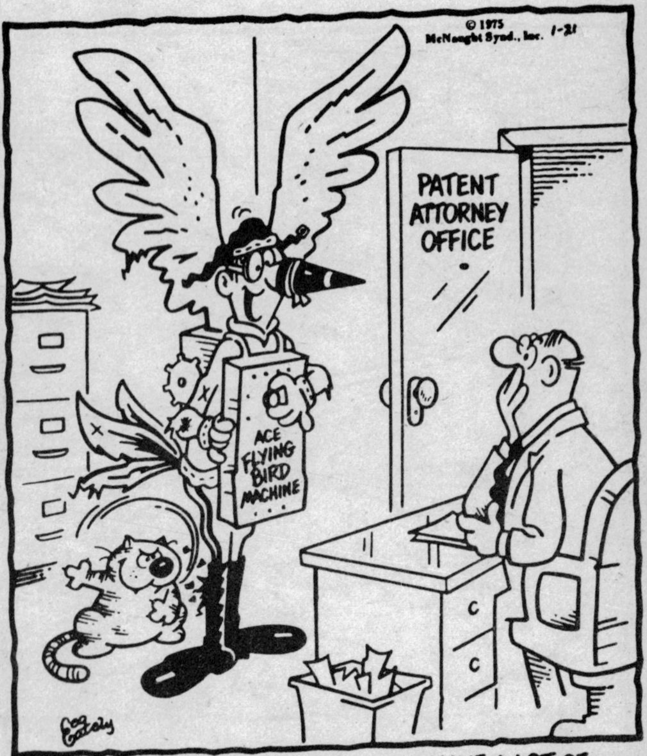
© 1975
McNaught Synd., Inc. 1-21
PATENT
ATTORNEY
OFFICE
ACE
FLYING
BIRD
MACHINE

"IT WORKS LIKE A CHARM!... BUT I HAVE A LOT OF TROUBLE WITH CATS!"

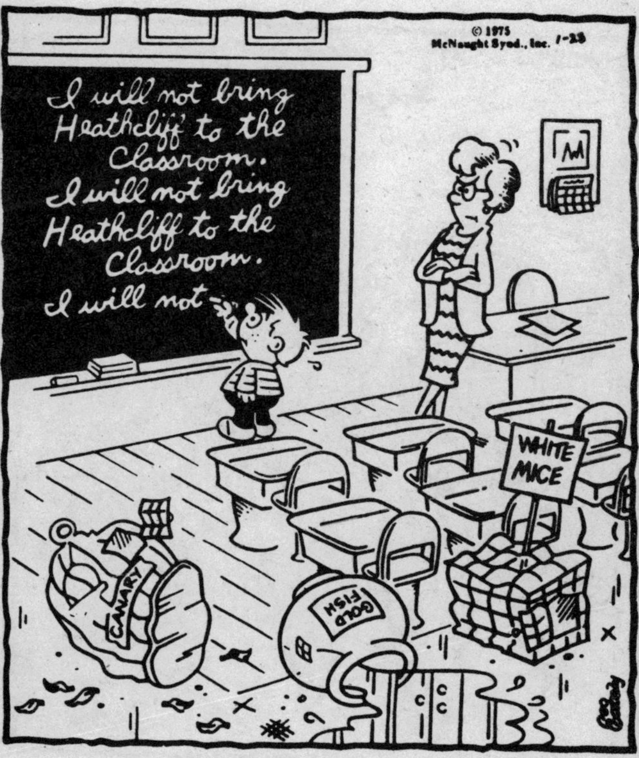

© 1975
McNaught Synd., Inc. 1-23
I will not bring Heathcliff to the Classroom.
I will not bring Heathcliff to the Classroom.
I will not
WHITE MICE
CANARY
GOLD FISH

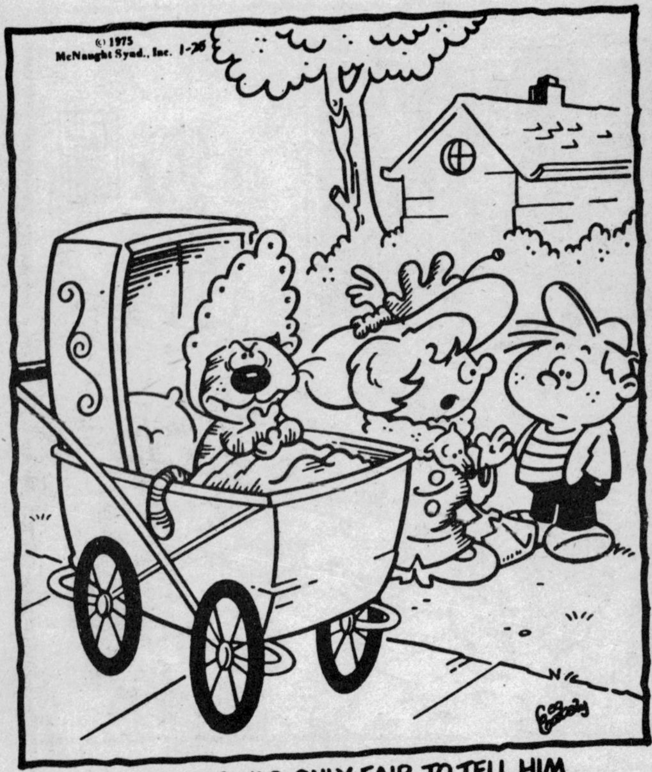
© 1975
McNaught Synd., Inc. 1-26

"I FELT IT WAS ONLY FAIR TO TELL HIM HE'S ADOPTED."

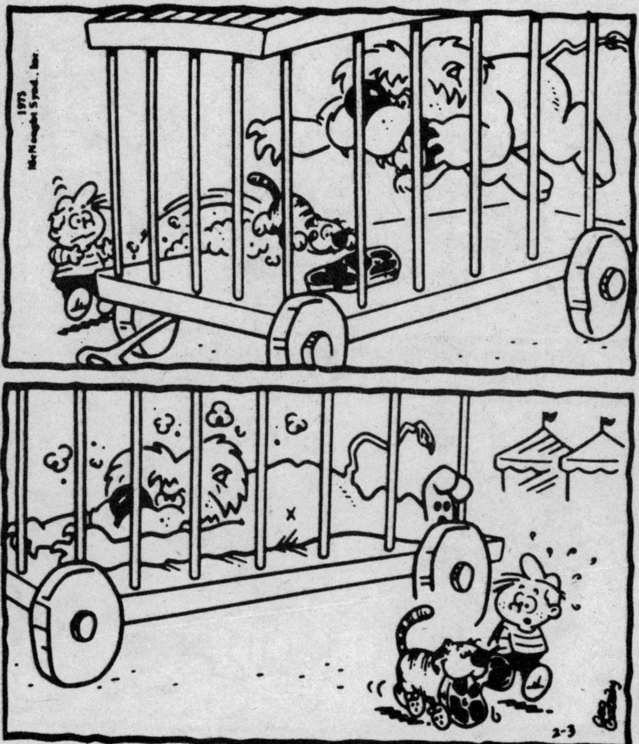
2-3

"OKAY... NOW YOU HAVE **EIGHT** LIVES LEFT!"

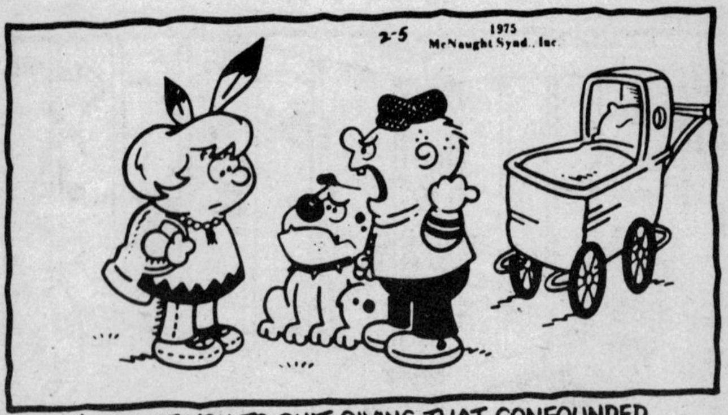
2-5
1975
McNaught Synd., Inc.

"I WANT YOU TO QUIT GIVING THAT CONFOUNDED HEATHCLIFF RIDES IN YOUR DOLL CARRIAGE!"

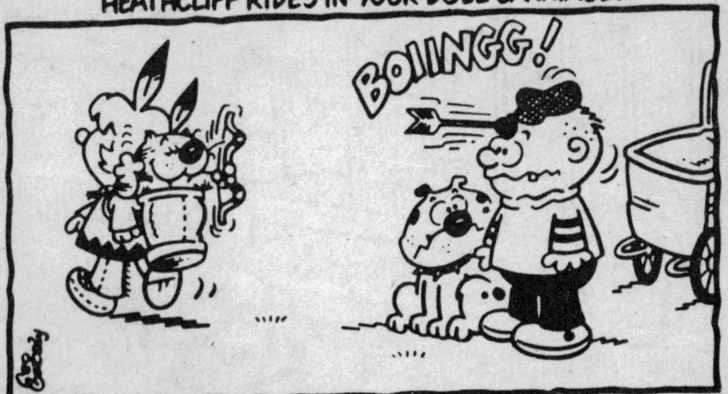
BOIINGG!

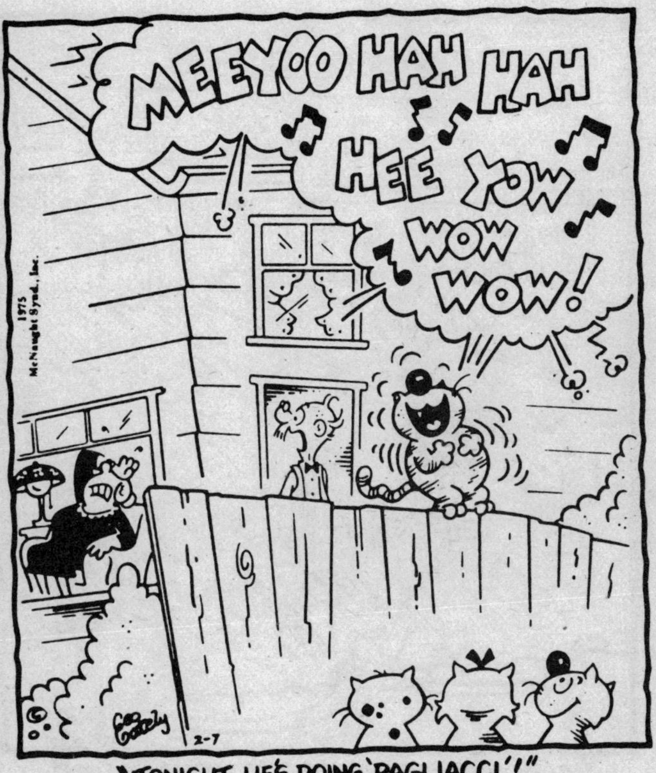
MEEYOO HAH HAH
HEE YOW
WOW
WOW!
1975
McNaught Synd., Inc.
2-7

"TONIGHT, HE'S DOING 'PAGLIACCI'!"

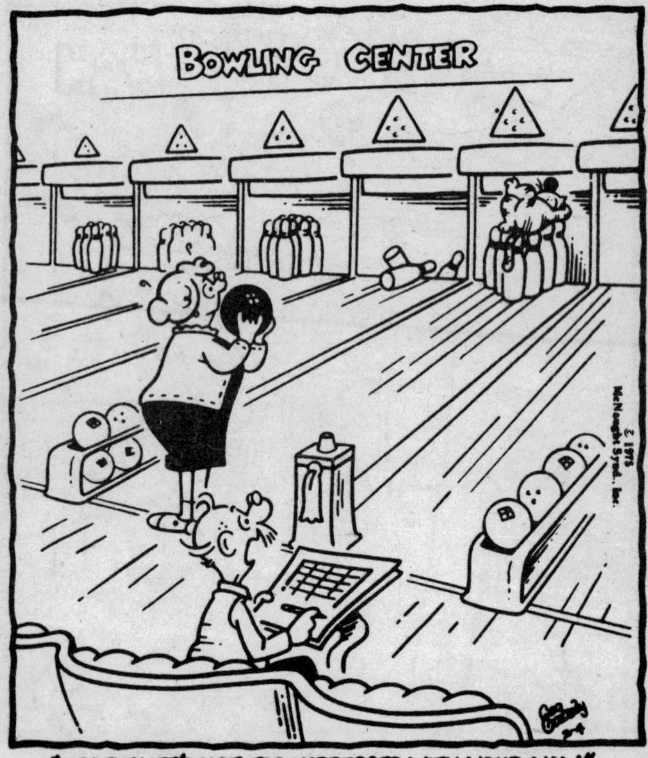
BOWLING CENTER
© 1975 McNaught Synd., Inc.

"HEATHCLIFF'S NOT TOO IMPRESSED WITH YOUR AIM!"

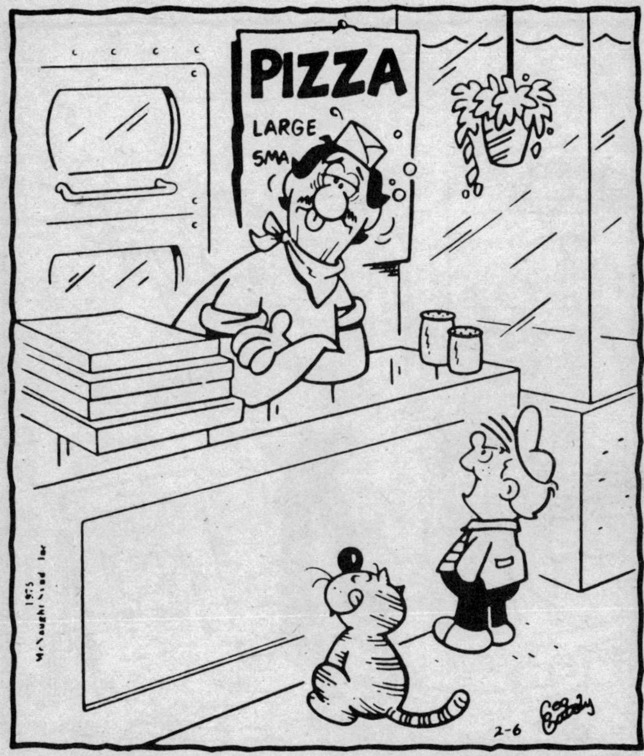
PIZZA
LARGE
SMA
1975 McNaught Synd Inc
2-6

"TWO PIES TO GO... ONE WITH PEPPERONI AND ONE WITH FISH HEADS."

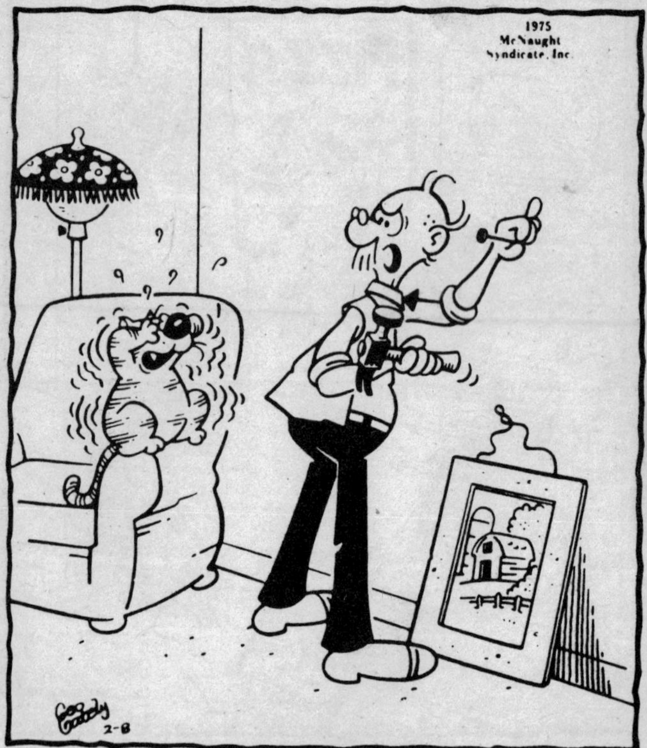
1975
McNaught
Syndicate, Inc.

"CUT THAT OUT!"

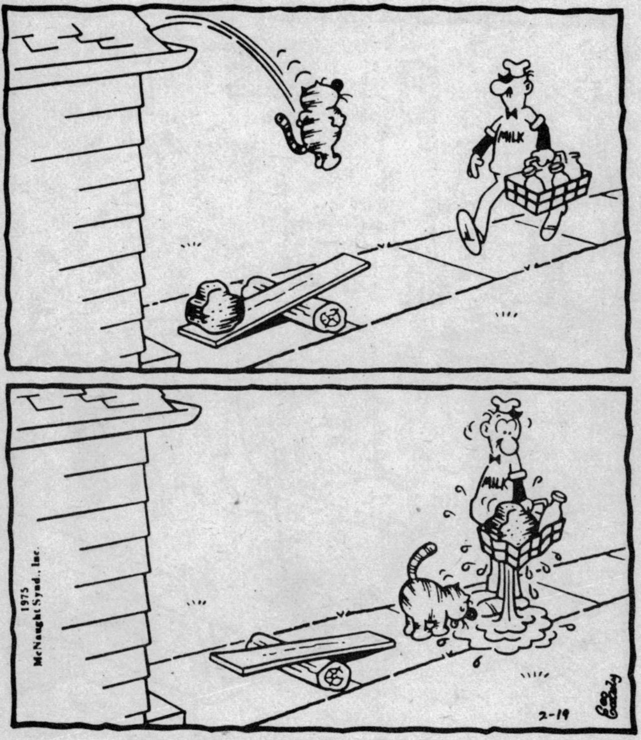
MILK
MILK
1975
McNaught Synd., Inc.
2-19

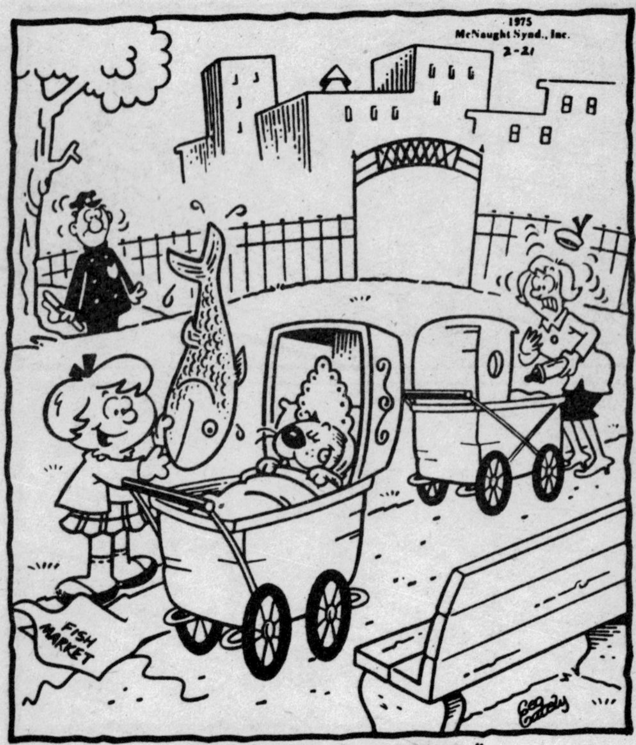

1975
McNaught Synd., Inc.
2-21
FISH MARKET

" TIME FOR DIN-DIN, BABY."

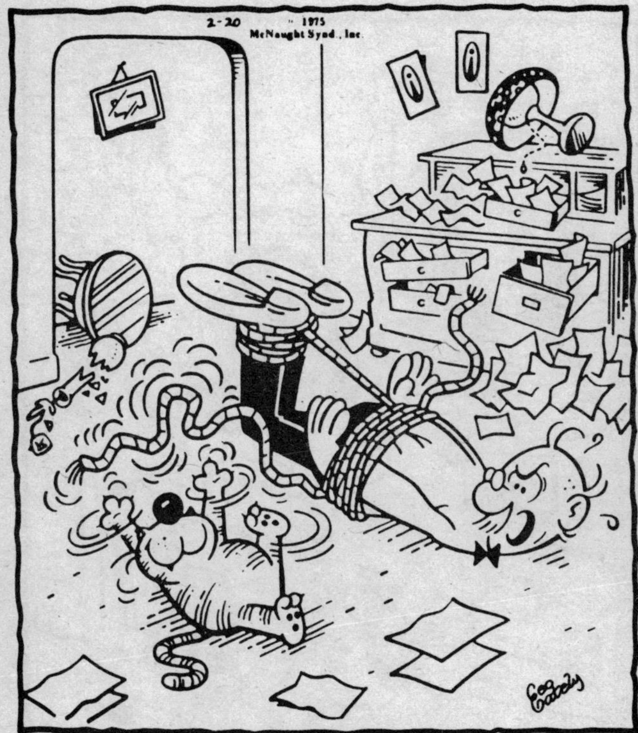
2-20 © 1975
McNaught Synd., Inc.

"GO FOR HELP, DUMMY!"

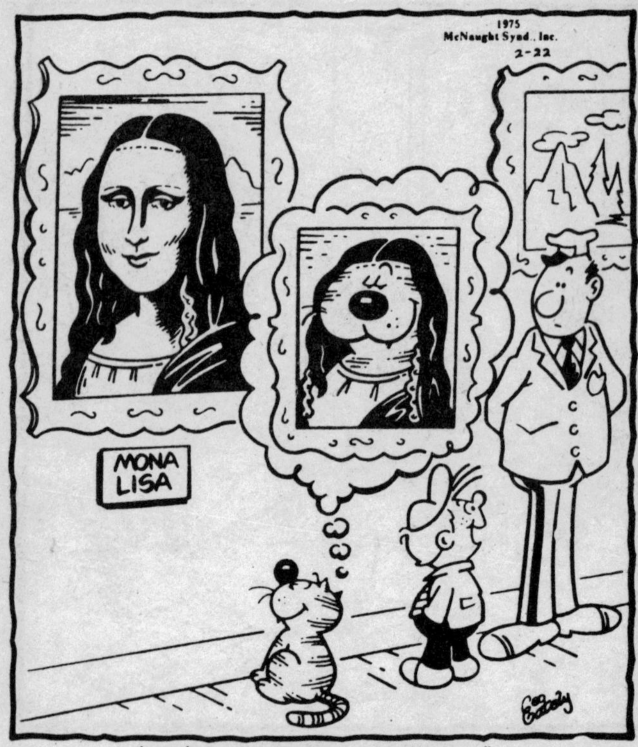
1975
McNaught Synd., Inc.
2-22
MONA
LISA

"HE'S VERY FOND OF DA VINCI."

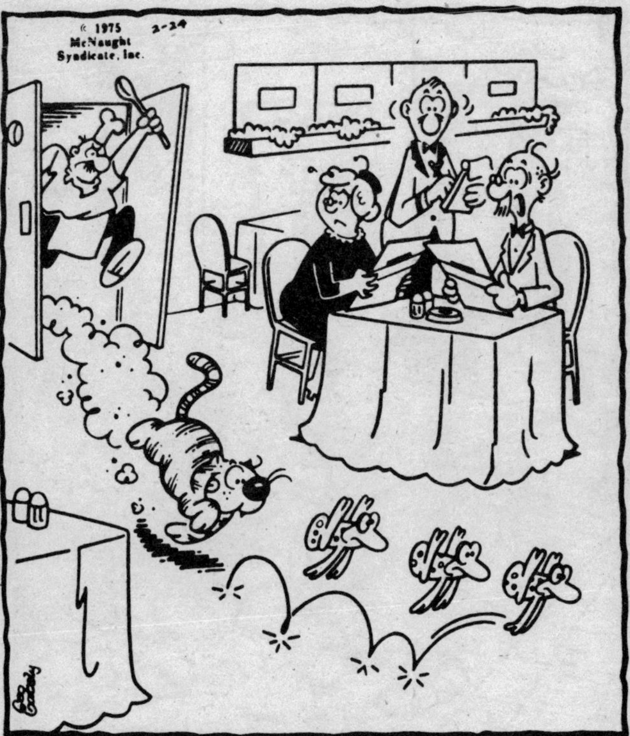
© 1975
McNaught
Syndicate, Inc.
2-24

"CANCEL THOSE FROG'S LEGS!"

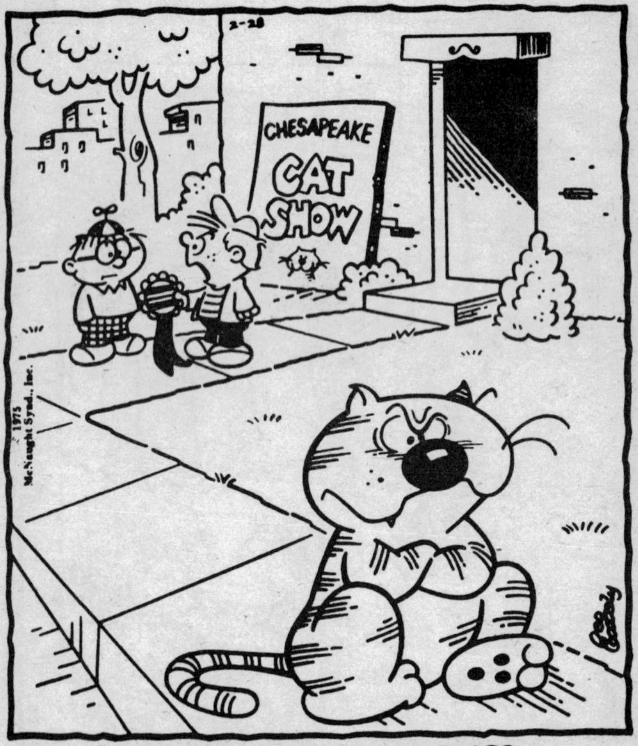
2-28
CHESAPEAKE
CAT
SHOW
© 1975 McNaught Synd., Inc.

"HEATHCLIFF GOT A SPECIAL·AWARD... 'BEST ALLEYCAT IN SHOW'."

"OH, YOU MIGHT BE ABLE TO SHAKE HIM OUT OF A TREE... ...BUT HE ALWAYS LANDS ON HIS FEET."

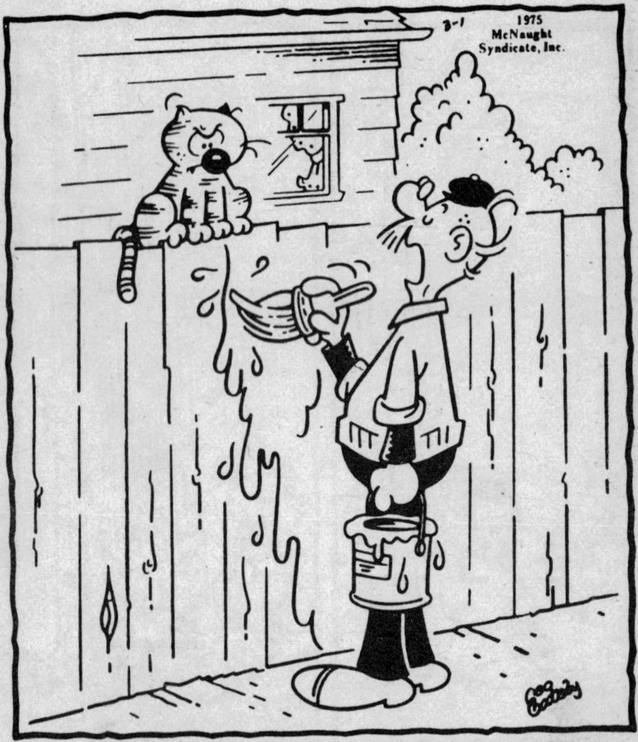
3-1
1975
McNaught
Syndicate, Inc.

"YOU'LL HAVE TO POSTPONE THE CONCERT UNTIL YOUR STAGE DRIES."

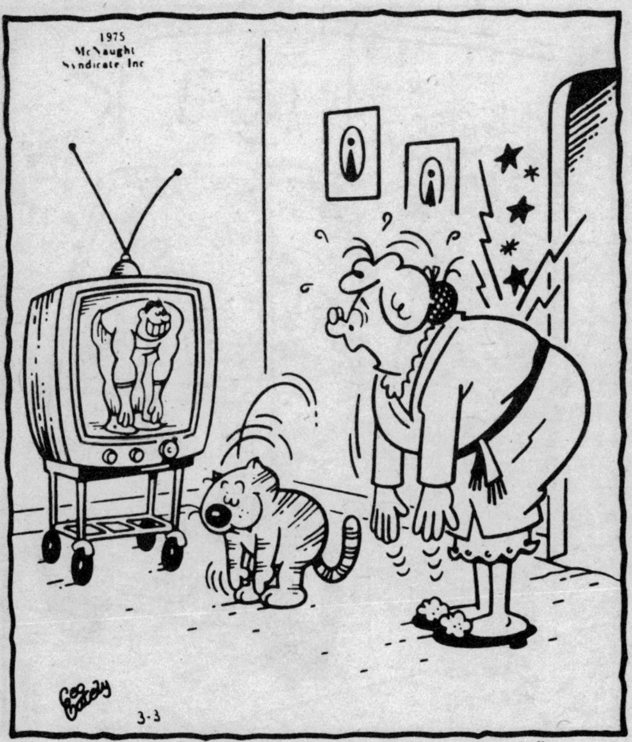
1975
McNaught
Syndicate, Inc
3-3
"I KNOW **YOU** CAN TOUCH YOUR TOES!!"

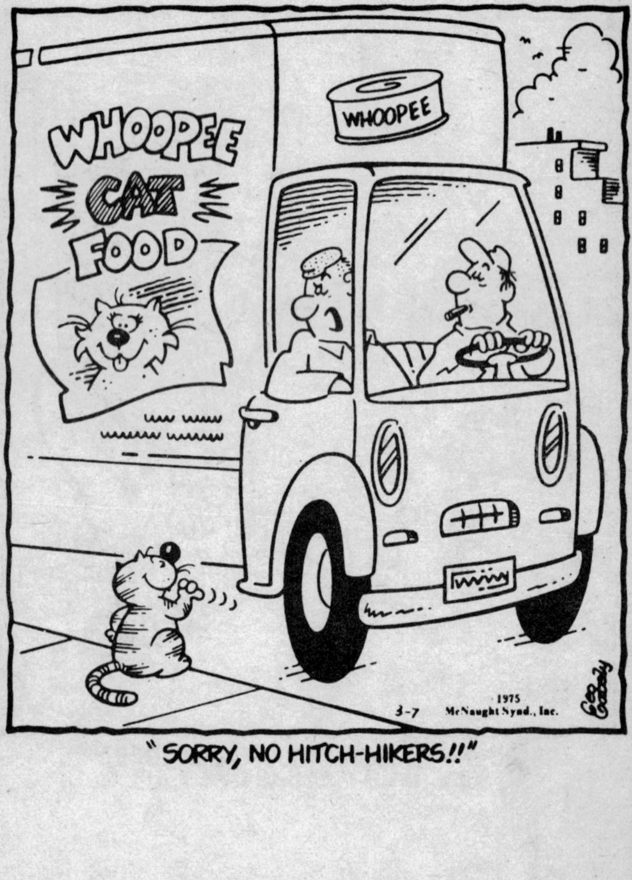
WHOOPEE
CAT
FOOD
WHOOPEE
3-7
© 1975 McNaught Synd., Inc.

"SORRY, NO HITCH-HIKERS!!"

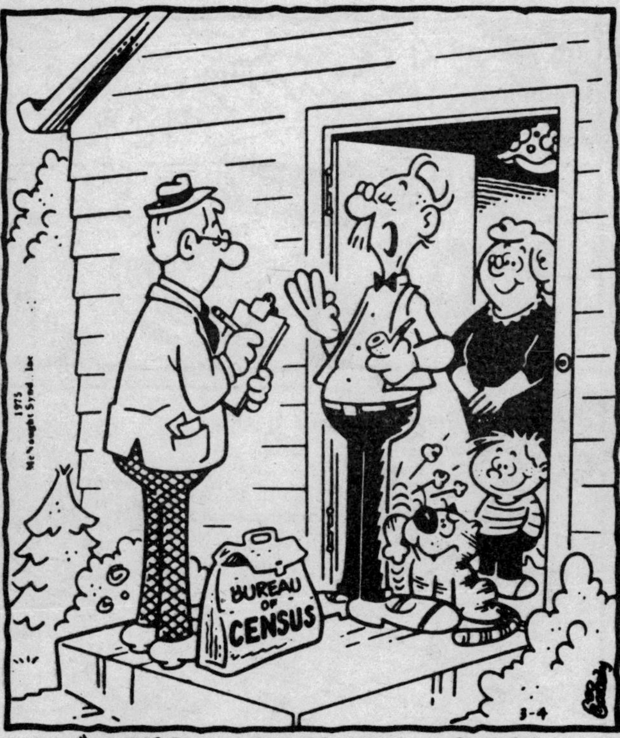
BUREAU
OF
CENSUS
3-4

"THREE PEOPLE RESIDE HERE... ALTHOUGH SOMETIMES IT SEEMS LIKE FOUR."

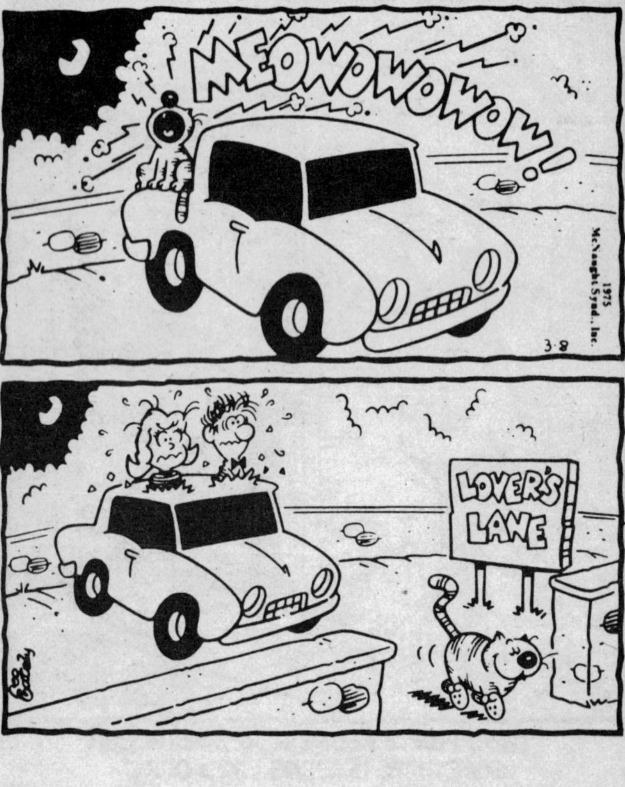
MEOWOWOWOWOW!
1975 McNaught Synd., Inc.
3·8
LOVER'S LANE

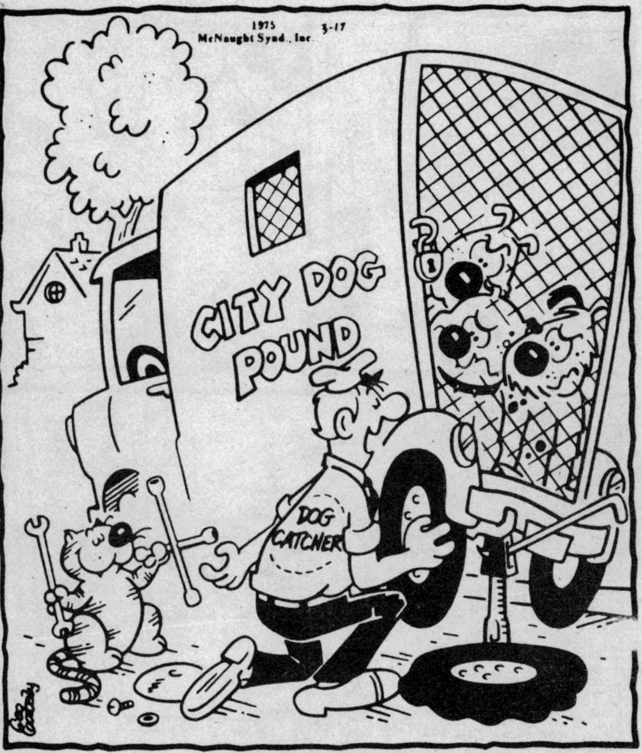
1975 McNaught Synd., Inc. 3-17
CITY DOG POUND
DOG CATCHER

"LUGWRENCH..."

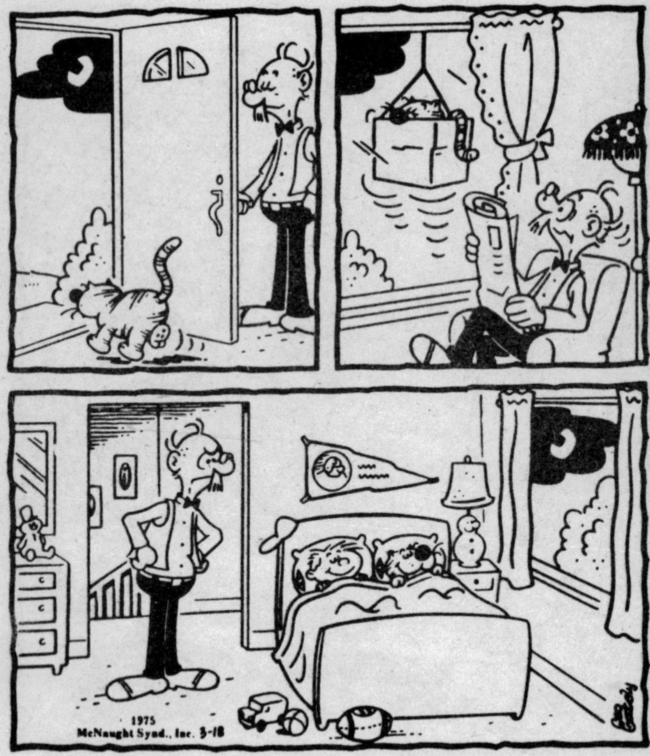
1975
McNaught Synd., Inc. 3-18

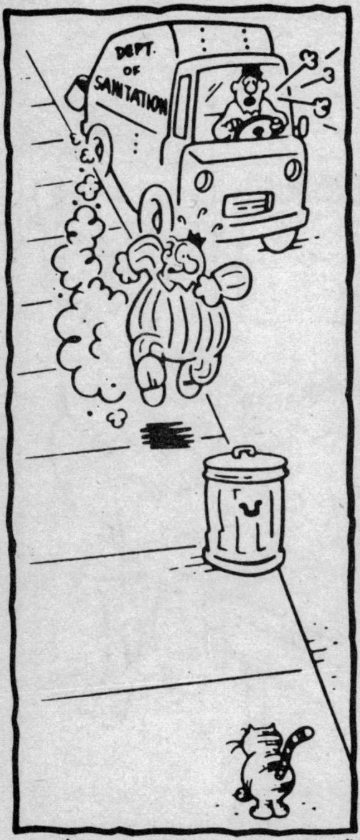
DEPT. OF SANITATION

"FASTER, CLANCY! FASTER!!"

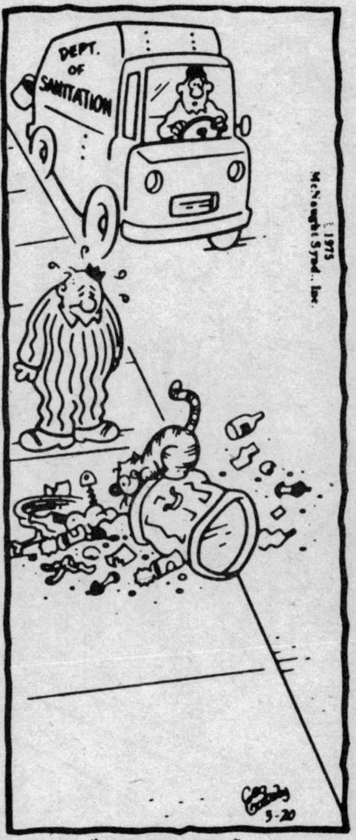
DEPT. OF SANITATION
© 1975 McNaught Synd., Inc.
5-20

"TOO LATE."

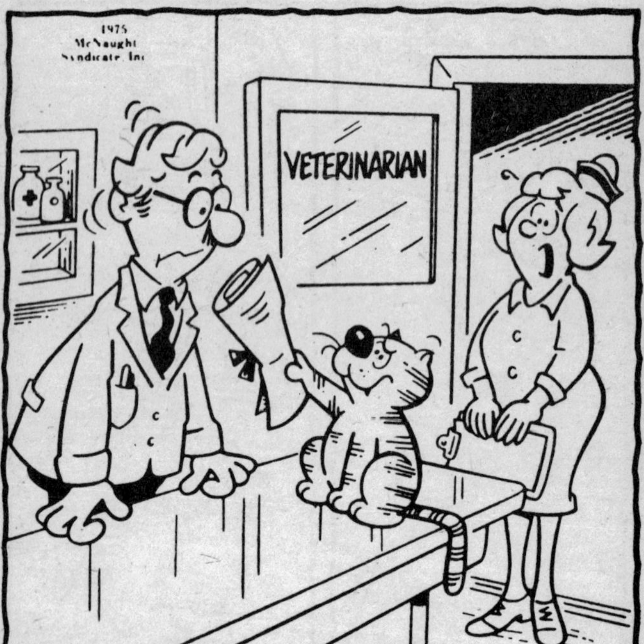
1975
McNaught
Syndicate, Inc
VETERINARIAN
3-22

"I THINK HE'S SUING YOU FOR MALPRACTICE!"

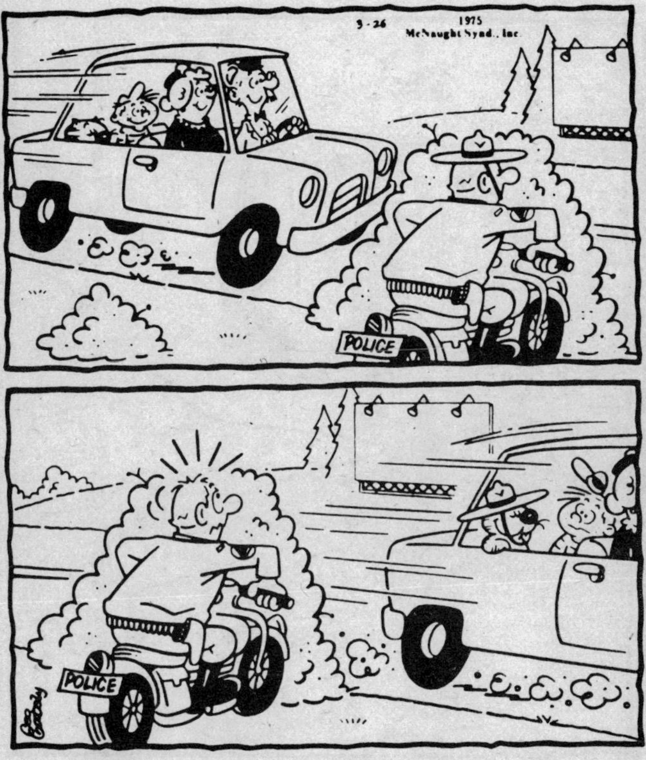
3-26
1975
McNaught Synd., Inc.
POLICE
POLICE

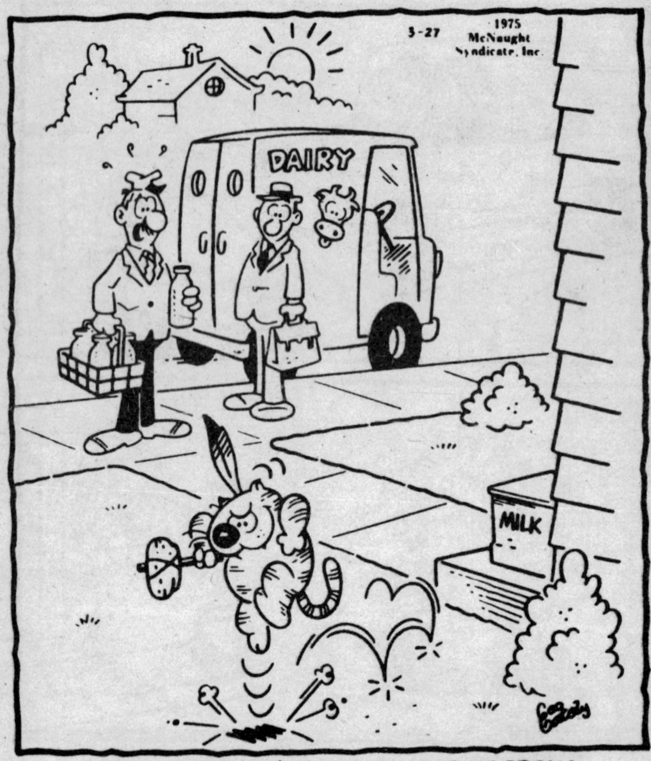
3-27
1975
McNaught
Syndicate, Inc.
DAIRY
MILK

"I JUST KNOW HE'S GOING TO MAKE ME BREAK A BOTTLE!... HE'S PERFORMING HIS 'MILK DANCE'!"

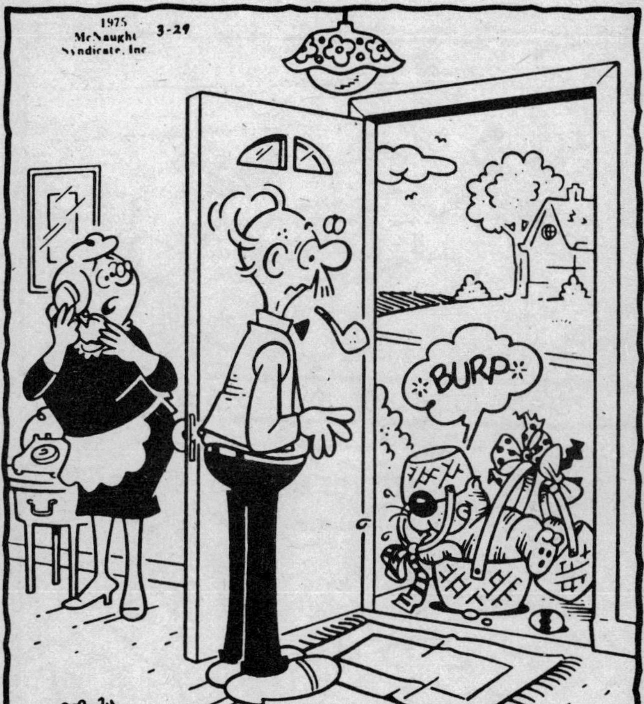
1975
McNaught
Syndicate, Inc
3-29
BURP

"IT'S 'SARAH'S SWEET SHOP'... SOMETHING ABOUT HEATHCLIFF RIFLING EASTER BASKETS!"

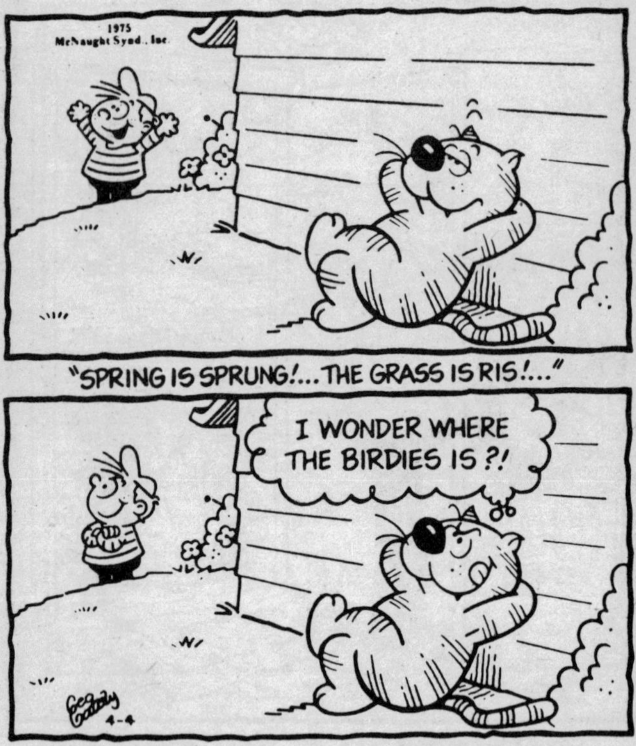
1975
McNaught Synd., Inc.
"SPRING IS SPRUNG!... THE GRASS IS RIS!..."
I WONDER WHERE THE BIRDIES IS ?!
4-4

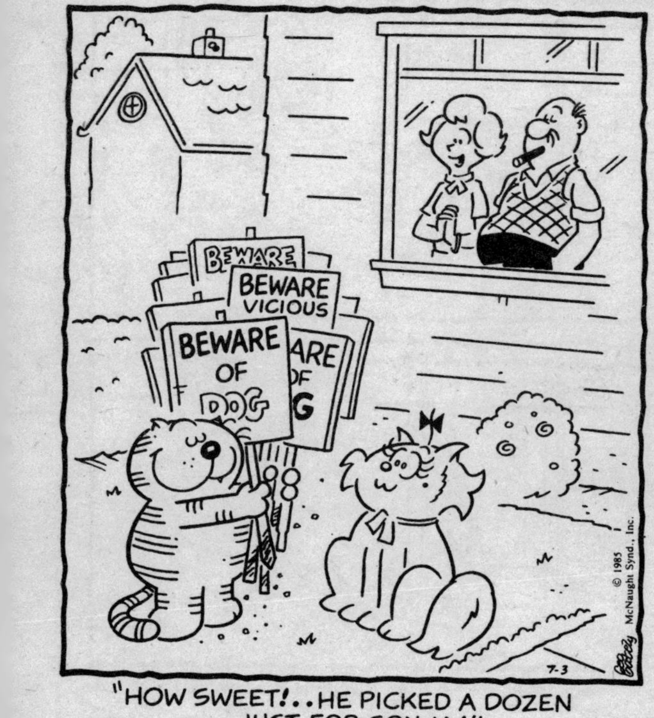
BEWARE
BEWARE
VICIOUS
BEWARE
OF
DOG
© 1985 McNaught Synd., Inc.
7-3
"HOW SWEET!..HE PICKED A DOZEN
JUST FOR SONJA!"

GRAN'MA'S
GRAN'MA'S
© 1985 McNaught Synd., Inc.
7-6

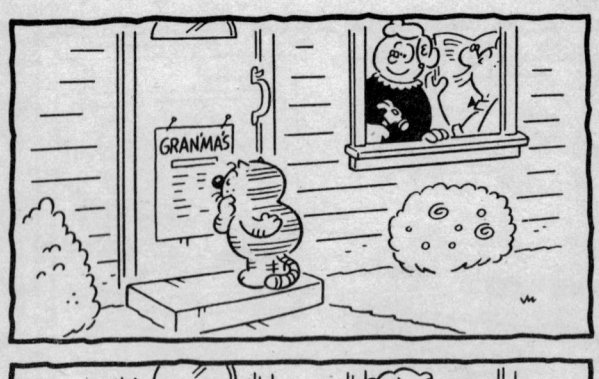

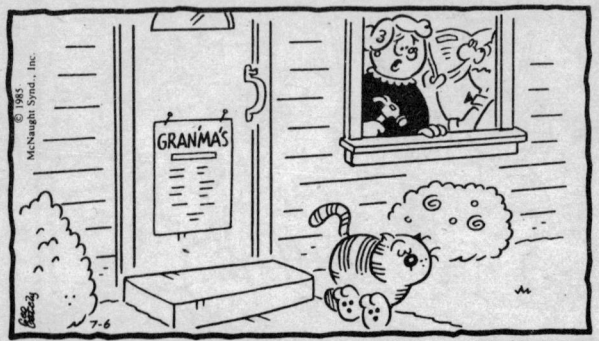

"HE DOESN'T LIKE TONIGHT'S MENU!"

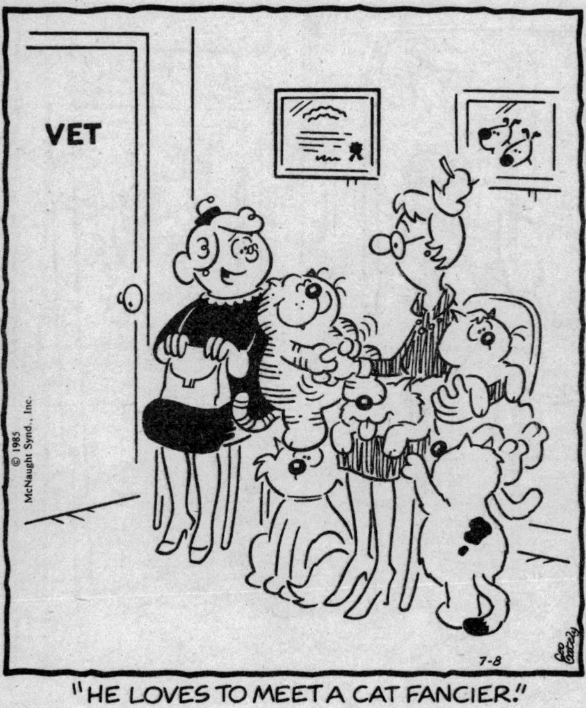
VET
© 1985
McNaught Synd., Inc.
7-8

"HE LOVES TO MEET A CAT FANCIER!"

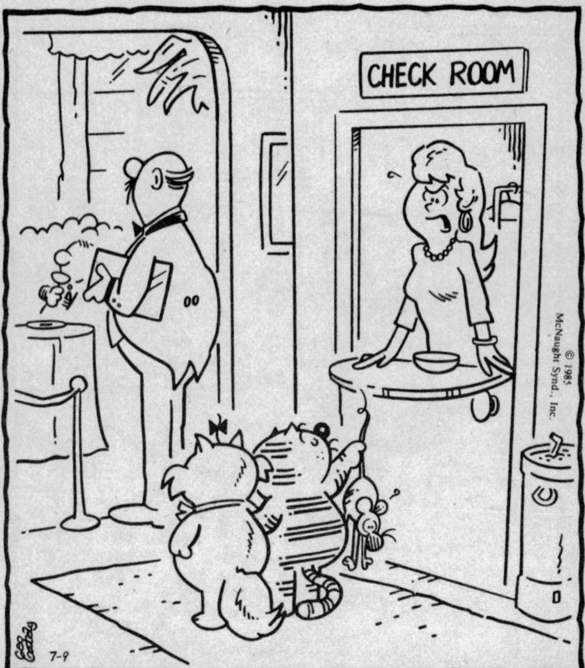
CHECK ROOM
© 1985 McNaught Synd., Inc.
7-9

"HATS AND COATS ONLY!!"

PAY TOLL
© 1985 McNaught Synd., Inc.
7-10

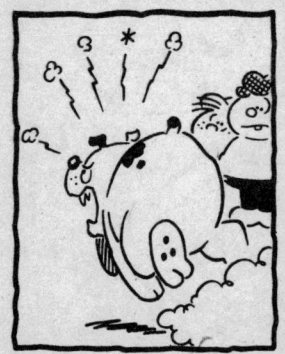

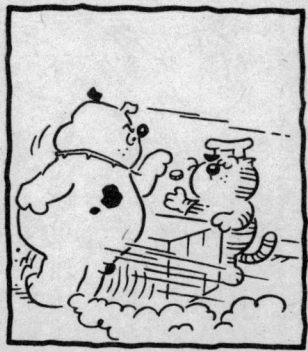

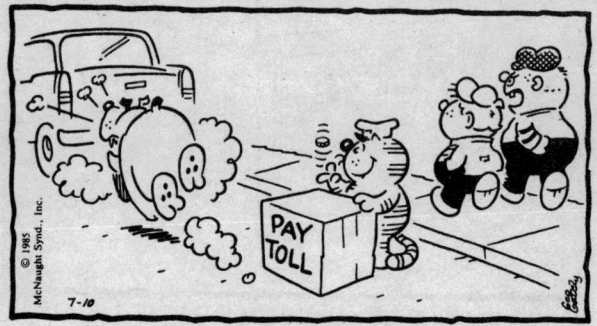

"IT'S COSTING SPIKE A FORTUNE TO CHASE CARS!"

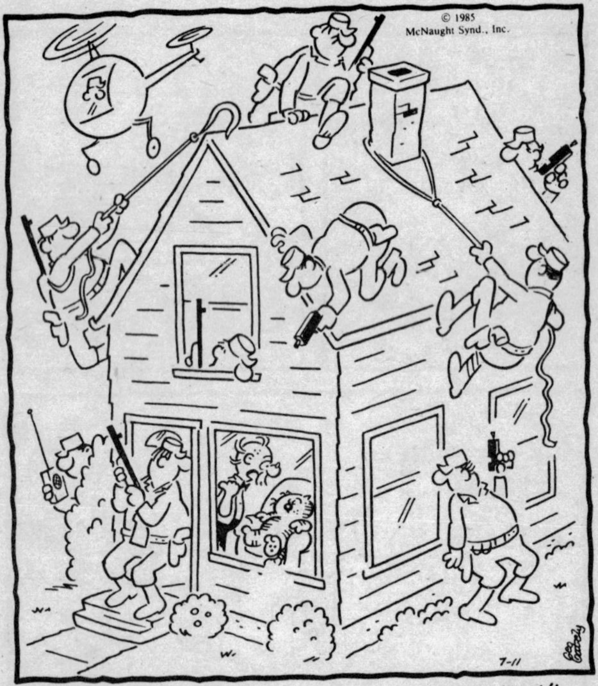
© 1985
McNaught Synd., Inc.
7-11

"THE SWAT TEAM WOULD LIKE TO SEE YOU!"

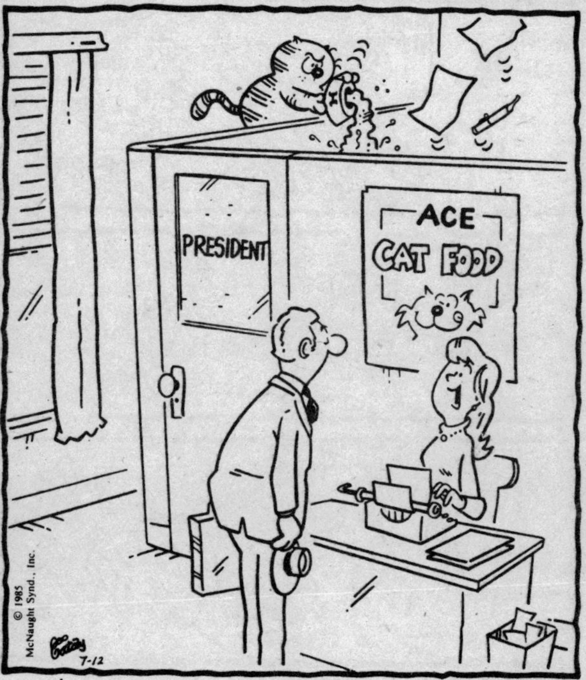
PRESIDENT
ACE
CAT FOOD
© 1985
McNaught Synd., Inc.
7-12

"HE'S HAVING LUNCH IN HIS OFFICE."

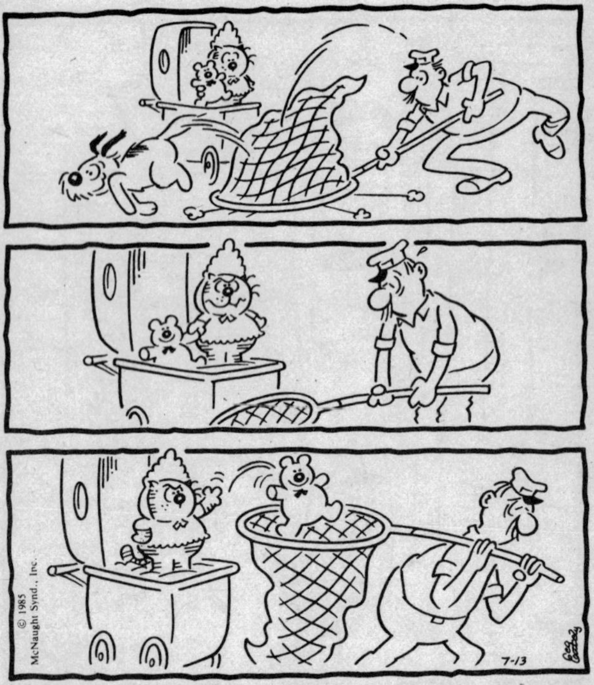
© 1985
McNaught Synd., Inc.
7-13